ABOUT CANADA
CHILDREN AND YOUTH

Bernard Schissel

About Canada Series

Fernwood Publishing • Halifax & Winnipeg

Editing & design: Brenda Conroy
Cover design: John van der Woude
Printed and bound in Canada by Hignell Book Printing

Published in Canada by Fernwood Publishing
32 Oceanvista Lane, Black Point, Nova Scotia, B0J 1B0
and 748 Broadway Avenue, Winnipeg, MB R3G 0X3
www.fernwoodpublishing.ca

Fernwood Publishing Company Limited gratefully acknowledges the financial support of the Government of Canada through the Canada Book Fund, the Canada Council for the Arts, the Nova Scotia Department of Tourism and Culture, the Manitoba Department of Culture, Heritage and Tourism under the Manitoba Publishers Marketing Assistance Program and the Province of Manitoba, through the Book Publishing Tax Credit, for our publishing program.

Library and Archives Canada Cataloguing in Publication

Schissel, Bernard, 1950-
Children and youth / Bernard Schissel.

(About Canada)
Includes bibliographical references.
ISBN 978-1-55266-434-6 (bound).–ISBN 978-1-55266-412-4 (pbk.)

1. Children's rights–Canada. 2. Youth–Civil rights–Canada. 3. Children–Canada–Social conditions. 4. Youth–Canada–Social conditions. I. Title.
II. Series: About Canada series

HQ792.C3S35 2011   323.3'520971   C2010-908044-0

CONTENTS

To Ben:
In hopes of a safe and just world
for children and youth

.

Introduction

THE RIGHTS OF CHILDREN

It should be a straightforward task to describe the state of children and youth in Canada. We are, in relative terms, a highly developed society in which democratic rights and protections are supposed to accrue to everyone. We would assume that young people receive rights and protections equal to or greater than anyone else, given our collective belief that young people represent the future. However, the situation of children and youth in Canada is bleaker than is commonly admitted, in both absolute and relative terms. The absolute condition of young people is a barometer of how well we protect our offspring. The relative condition is a barometer of how well our good intentions extend to all children, those living with privilege and those living without.

There are deep contradictions in the public perception about children and youth. The "vulnerable child principle" is one that we hold in common and that generates considerable fear among adults for children, especially their own children. State welfare agencies assume, for example, that given their age and lack of experience, young people are especially vulnerable to the predatory nature of society. The "competent child principle," on the other hand, is based on the premise that young people have competencies that need to be fostered and that their independence is to be encouraged. Parents strive to raise independent, self-assured and fearless children who can step out into the world without hesitancy. Our bipolar view of children and youth in Canadian society creates problems not only for parents but also for social policy makers who attempt to create and run institutions that aid in the protection and development of kids. Unfortunately, a third view springs from the view of the child as competent. Political campaigns, and ensuing social and justice policy, are often based on the belief that children can be too competent, that they can pose a threat to community well-being and security. The vulnerable, the competent and the threatening child are all images that have informed youth criminal justice policy in Canada to varying degrees at various historical periods.

This book takes us on a complex and contradictory journey of discovery into a world that, on one hand, craves to protect the young and innocent and, on the other, is dismissive or, at worst, vengeful. Some of our laws are clearly intended to protect the young from predatory adults, and yet for centuries, children have suffered abuse and neglect in formalized school systems and, more distressingly, in their own families. We know that children and youth are often the victims of war. We stand in abhorrence of war, and yet we think nothing of encouraging young people to enter the military, heralding war-zone service as a tribute to youthful social engagement.

When we compile empirical evidence regarding the heath of the young, the exploitation of the young by the corporate world, the abuse of the rights of the young in our justice system, the rigidity of some education systems and the position of young people on the socio-economic strata, we find that our expressed desire to protect the young is somewhat of a conceit. We discover that young people in Canada and worldwide are not privileged—in fact, they often lack the basic human rights that we suppose accrue to everyone. The story of Omar Khadr is significant at this time in Canadian history because it illustrates clearly how far we fall from human grace when politics overrides humanity. Although the Khadr case is complicated by issues of war and sovereignty, the reality is that Canada essentially abandoned a fifteen-year-old citizen to the political demands of another country in abrogation of child rights.

Children's rights, most of which are universally agreed upon, form the framework for the discussions in this book. I explore the state of children and youth in Canada by describing the social and economic nature of Canada's young in the contexts of the *Charter of Rights and Freedoms* and the *United Nations Convention on the Rights of the Child*, to which Canada is a signatory. These important agreements articulate the basic rights of food, clothing and shelter, freedom from ill-health and freedom from harm, among others.

Although this book is directed primarily to Canadian society, it is impossible to understand the situation of Canadian young people outside of the global situation of young people. In the West, we often hear news reports of children being exploited in troubled spots in other parts of the world. Rightly, our hearts go out to the young people and their families. Ironically, such compassion for children suffering outside of our borders often masks an antipathy toward Canadian children and youth, especially disadvantaged youth. This book is a study of the best of care and the worst of care, of good intentions and less than good outcomes.

My purpose in this book is simple. I am concerned with how we respond to the following United Nations' declaration:

> Parties shall take all appropriate legislative, administrative, social and educational measures to protect the child from all forms of physical or mental violence, injury or abuse, neglect or negligent treatment, maltreatment or exploitation, including sexual abuse, while in the care of parent(s), legal guardian(s) or any other person who has the care of the child.

The statement is uncomplicated in its moral position and grounded in an unassailable ethic of care many would argue is primordial. This book is a report card on how we measure up to these words and intentions.

In any discussions of children's rights, one of the constants in the bureaucracy we have created to deal with children and youth in Canada is the vigilance and dedication of many adults who care for children. Such people are exemplified by teachers, for example, who spend extra hours in innovative schools program for children at risk, youth workers in the justice system, who work beyond their mandate to care for kids who have no place to live, and justice officials, who practise discretion to make sure that young people in trouble with the law are treated with kindness and support, not only for ethical reasons but also as a foundation for healing. It is also important to realize that many of those in charge of children and youth in society earn insufficient wages given the importance of their work and that they often work in the context of scarce resources and without much political support, and often aggressive political opposition. This book is also a reminder that their plight is not an enviable one.

Chapter 1

FREEDOM FROM WANT

As a society that prides itself on its quality of life and its general ethos of caring for others, we generally abhor the fact that some children live in poverty. Moreover, our concern clearly extends beyond the borders of Canada to impoverished children in the developing world. According to Statistics Canada's 2007 Survey on Giving, Volunteering and Participating,[1] next to religious donations, Canadians give more to international aid programs than to anything else, and the majority of these programs are directed at children. Our collective concern, our group sense of right and wrong, is somewhat tarnished, however, by the reality that there are pockets of child poverty in Canada that equal the poverty in many poorer countries throughout the world. Why have we not been as committed to repairing the ravages of poverty on children and their families within Canadian borders as we have been elsewhere? It would seem morally reasonable that we should want to work toward a society, our own society, in which child poverty and indeed all poverty in our country disappears.

While the elimination of child poverty may seem like an impossible goal, or at best an ethical ideal, there are countries, such as Sweden and Norway, that have rates of child poverty that are almost negligible. The information in Figure 1.1 makes it clear that some countries do much better than others when it comes to eliminating child poverty. Significantly, though, poverty levels do not seem to be related to the inherent wealth of a country, since Canada and the United States, wealthy countries by international standards, have relatively high levels of child poverty. The United States has child poverty at levels similar to Mexico and Turkey, and much higher than Greece. Some of the European countries of equal or lower economic

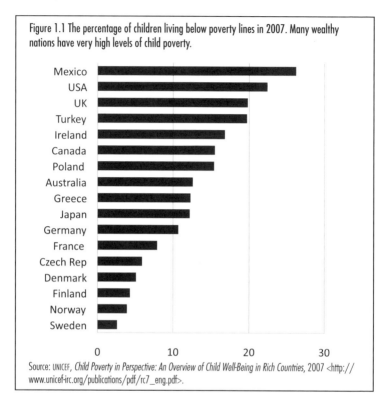

Figure 1.1 The percentage of children living below poverty lines in 2007. Many wealthy nations have very high levels of child poverty.

Source: UNICEF, *Child Poverty in Perspective: An Overview of Child Well-Being in Rich Countries,* 2007 <http://www.unicef-irc.org/publications/pdf/rc7_eng.pdf>.

well-being, however, have quite low levels of child poverty. Differences aside, the quality of life for children is deteriorating worldwide.

Canada in a Global Context

Any serious discussion of the elimination of poverty in Canada must consider the worldwide context. The globalized modern world is much different from the world of the past. It is now more integrated and less defined by national boundaries. Technology permits North American industries to outsource much of their work to countries throughout the world. In fact, major multinational corporations rarely acknowledge a national place of residence, except for corporate headquarters. This trend, coupled with the growing elimination of barriers to trade, has resulted in the expansion of economic and political power for multinational corporations, many of which have economies larger than some countries. What this means for the welfare of young people is that many countries without labour regulations use children and youth as cheap workers as they compete in a global market. In fact, when First World trade and finance organizations like the World Trade Organization (WTO) and the International Monetary Fund (IMF) demand that developing countries abide by free enterprise/free market principles as a condition of financing, they create the conditions under which young citizens get exploited. The free market model demands a brand of fiscal responsibility that insists on spending cuts in health, social housing and education. Sadly, as the developed and the developing worlds converge under the global tutelage of the WTO, IMF and others, child poverty increases across the globe. The World Bank Report of 2000 entitled *The World Development Report 2000/2001: Attacking Poverty*[2] and the more recent UNICEF Report Card 9, *The Children Left Behind*[3] confirm this reality for children living in poverty in developed as well as developing countries. Ironically, the sentiment in the western world towards Third World child poverty is most often condemnatory of national and local custom in so-called "underdeveloped" countries, not international policies.

The UNICEF *Innocenti Report Card 7* provides a picture of international child poverty. This report card ranks six specific and important dimensions of child well-being in the world's richer countries, including Canada. These dimensions frame the discussions in this book. In Table 1.1, a white background indicates a place in the top third of the table; light grey denotes the middle third and dark grey the bottom third.

While Canada does well with respect to material well-being (based on family income and employment) and education, we do poorly in regard to preventing injurious behaviours, including substance abuse, violence and other forms of risk, and in regard to maintaining children's health and their satisfaction with their lives. In an overall assessment of child well-being, we rank in the middle, well behind many European countries. How do we explain that as one of the wealthiest countries in the world, our record on child well-being is, at best, average? Further, how do we explain the inconsistencies across dimensions of well-being? Why are Canadian children at risk relative to other countries, especially with respect to health, safety and security, and their own belief in their well-being? In general, what we need to reflect on is that our concern for poor children in other parts of the world, while com-

Table 1.1 Several dimensions of child well-being in the world's richer countries. As with child poverty, the richest countries do not have the best-off children.

Dimension		1	2	3	4	5	6
Dimensions of child well-being	Average ranking position (for all 6 dimensions)	Material well-being	Health and safety	Educational well-being	Family and peer relationships	Behaviours and risks	Subjective well-being
Netherlands	4.2	10	2	6	3	3	1
Sweden	5.0	1	1	5	15	1	7
Denmark	7.2	4	4	8	9	6	12
Finland	7.5	3	3	4	17	7	11
Spain	8.0	12	6	15	8	5	2
Switzerland	8.3	5	9	14	4	12	6
Norway	8.7	2	8	11	10	13	8
Italy	10.0	14	5	20	1	10	10
Ireland	10.2	19	19	7	7	4	5
Belgium	10.7	7	16	1	5	19	16
Germany	11.2	13	11	10	13	11	9
Canada	11.8	6	13	2	18	17	15
Greece	11.8	15	18	16	11	8	3
Poland	12.3	21	15	3	14	2	19
Czech Republic	12.5	11	10	9	19	9	17
France	13.0	9	7	18	12	14	18
Portugal	13.7	16	14	21	2	15	14
Austria	13.8	8	20	19	16	16	4
Hungary	14.5	20	17	13	6	18	13
United States	18.0	17	21	12	20	20	-
United Kingdom	18.2	18	12	17	21	21	20

Source: UNICEF, "Child Poverty in Perspective," *Innocenti Report Card 7*, 2007. Florence, Italy <www.unicef-irc.org/publications/pdf/rc7_eng.pdf>.

mendable, stands in contrast to our relatively poor record of national action for Canadian children who live in conditions of poverty.

Like some other developed countries, Canada is characterized by labour market poverty, which results not primarily from lack of work but from family inability to derive a decent standard of living from labour wages. As the National Council of Welfare has repeatedly stated, the inability for some Canadian families to maintain an adequate standard of living from wage labour coupled with a decreasing levels of social spending since the 1990s results in continuing high rates of child poverty.[4] High rates of child poverty are especially high in single parent families, even though in Canada and the United States, approximately 70 percent of single mothers work the equivalent of full-time for wages but remain below the poverty line.[5]

Understanding Child and Youth in Poverty in Canada

In our attempts to understand child poverty in Canadian society, it is important to keep in mind the substantial disparities that exist across regional and social categories (see Figure 1.2). The provincial patterns of poverty are somewhat counterintuitive. British Columbia, a historical "have" province, has the highest provincial rate of child poverty, followed by Manitoba, Saskatchewan and New Brunswick. Prince Edward Island and Newfoundland/Labrador, historical "have not" provinces, have the lowest rates of child poverty, along with resource rich Alberta. According to the National Council of Welfare,[6] within these provincial contexts, the highest rates of poverty occur for recent immigrants (33 percent), Aboriginal children (28 percent) and visible minority children (26 percent). The poverty rate for non-visible minority children is 12 percent and the overall rate is 18 percent. These comparative rates clearly show that children in marginalized groups are much more likely to be poor than their mainstream counterparts. Explanations for the substantial disparities by region and race are found, in part, in the history of Canada.

Canadian History, Resource Development and Poverty

The history of Canada is characterized not only by exploitation of natural resources but also the deliberate or inadvertent exploitation of peoples and cultures. Canada has historically been aggressive in the extraction of raw materials from the North, including gas and oil, hydroelectricity, timber and minerals. Typically, primary resource industries extract and export either to

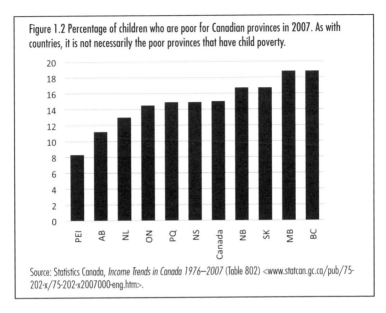

Figure 1.2 Percentage of children who are poor for Canadian provinces in 2007. As with countries, it is not necessarily the poor provinces that have child poverty.

Source: Statistics Canada, *Income Trends in Canada 1976–2007* (Table 802) <www.statcan.gc.ca/pub/75-202-x/75-202-x2007000-eng.htm>.

southern Canada or to elsewhere in the world. Industrialization is justified by the following rationale in the minds of policy makers and the public at large: industry creates wealth, which creates jobs, which improves the standard of living, which improves the quality of life. This economic reasoning seems logical and compelling. However, in Canada for over a hundred years, the benefits that were to accrue to local populations and economies have rarely happened, and when they have, the influences have been disruptive and short-lived. So, what happened to families and communities?

For the most part, people in local communities receive only menial jobs with low pay. Technical, service-based and professional jobs are filled by imported "southern labour" or outsourced. The infrastructural support (like schools, athletic facilities and health facilities) that is so essential to vi-able, sustainable communities is rarely put in place. When megaprojects like the James Bay hydro project in northern Quebec were completed, the jobs disappeared, except for highly specialized positions filled by outsiders. Not only are such communities left in an economic vacuum, but the geography is altered, the ecology is changed irrevocably, traditional cultures are disrupted, and what little infrastructural support there was vanishes. Traditional ways of living are no longer viable, and children and youth are caught between tradition and family, and the new reality of industrial development. We need only to observe the massive geographical, ecological and cultural change that has occurred in the northern Alberta tar sand area to understand how communities can never go back—and how quickly they change in the face of development. History has taught us that rapid change, especially in traditional communities, causes dysfunction and instability, and this is precisely what has happened in several areas in Canada. The rapid industrialization of traditional communities offers children and youth little in terms of future meaningful work and infrastructural support. Furthermore, the once solid extended family system that provided security and care for the young has been eroded as traditional ways of sustenance have disappeared and no local work takes their place. Family members commuting to the Alberta tar sands is now commonplace from places as far away as the Atlantic Provinces. The centralization of wealth and regional disparity has created the conditions under which people need to leave their homes, either temporarily or permanently, to survive.

The community of La Loche in northern Saskatchewan is an example of how a single act of industrialization can change a community forever, especially with respect to the young. The Government of Saskatchewan constructed a highway between La Loche and Fort McMurray to permit La Loche residents to take advantage of the tremendous economic potential in the tar sands. Local, provincial and national politicians heralded the road as a panacea for the problems of the north because the road would shorten the commute between Fort McMurray and La Loche from ten hours to just less than two. Political leaders collectively declared that the road and its attendant development potential would improve the quality of life and greatly improve economic development opportunities for northern residents. The reality, however, is different; La Loche now has a growing drug trade, a growing gang problem and a growing generation of disaffected youth. The La Loche situation is not unique: rapid change and development infuses traditional communities with new money and little infrastructural opportunity for community or personal development. Oil and gas development does just that — it generates short-term wealth with little or no investment in the long-term needs of the community. Long-term and social infrastructural investment in an area of finite natural resources is not of interest to investors.

Almost twenty years ago, journalist Geoffrey York (1992) wrote an influential book entitled *The Dispossessed: Life and Death in Native Canada*.[7] The importance of this book rests in its profound understanding of the linkages between rapid, unbridled industrialization of Canada's north and the impact of that industrialization on traditional communities. His argument is clear and well-defended: when a community suffers social, economic and geographical disruption, hopelessness and despair follow. He describes how, in northern Manitoba, rapid economic development led to the relocation of the Shamattawa Cree Nation. The community went from virtually no social pathology to a place where self-injury and substance abuse became normal, everyday activities. York describes how children and youth shared the despair of the adults in the community and fell prey to gasoline sniffing, one of the most dangerous of addictions. The young people responded in this way to try to normalize what had become a very dysfunctional, socially deteriorating community with a bleak future.

One way to try to understand the despair that young people feel is to visualize ourselves or our children in a context where there is nothing to look forward to in terms of work and occupational development, very little to do on a daily basis and very little hope of surviving in a world which demands skills and cultural assimilation. Those of us who live in functional worlds have access to healthy occupational and leisure pursuits, which generate a sense of optimism for ourselves and our offspring. Such is not the case in many forgotten communities in Canada. When a people are shunted off to the margins of society, either through socio-political neglect or economic exploitation and relocation, the damages are extreme and affect children and youth directly and quickly. The additional reality for children and families in exploited communities is that they often migrate to major cities to find better lives. Most often, such migrants end up in inner city areas looking for people with whom they can form a community. Whether it is life on an inner city street or life in a socio-economically damaged Northern Aboriginal community, Canadian children and youth in these all but forgotten places are at great risk, and the physical and emotional suffering they experience follows them to adulthood. And, the suffering of each generation passes on to the next.

Geographical Isolation

An explanation for how caring people like Canadians forget the suffering of children within their own borders has to do with population isolation and geography. As we will see later in this book, many poor kids live in invisible areas, the geographically isolated north or the socially isolated inner city. As noted above, the communities that are most historically disadvantaged,

Still Waiting: A Cree Community on James Bay Has Been Fighting for a New Elementary School for More than a Decade.

This place is not a real school. Eleven rough buildings stand in a narrow strip between the fenced contamination site and an airstrip. In poor condition, the gloomy structures do not resemble anything you could describe as a school.

I arrived at recess time. Kids poured out of the squat classrooms to play tag, kick a ball or climb up on a fire hydrant to play King of the Castle. This barren yard is their playground — no swings, no slides, no monkey bars, no baseball diamond or soccer field. In deepest winter, students pull on parkas, snow pants and boots to walk to the community centre for phys. ed. Their school has no gym.

There is no library, no cafeteria, no art room, no music room. There are no heated corridors between the scattered classrooms. Every day, children and teachers walk inside and outside — inside and outside, inside and outside — through blizzards, ice fog, sleet and thunderstorms. Maintenance workers move a rough wooden ramp to a different portable every year to allow access to a disabled student as he moves through the grades.

In the past five years, Canada has made the construction of schools one of its signature projects in Afghanistan. Canadians plan to spend millions of dollars to build 50 new schools, with 16 already built and another 27 under construction. So why doesn't Attawapiskat have a new elementary school yet? It is the closing month of 2010 after all.

Source: Linda Goyette, "Still Waiting: A Cree community on James Bay has been fighting for a new elementary school for more than a decade. How Indian and Northern Affairs Canada is failing the next generation," *Canadian Geographic*, December 2010, pp. 48–64.

the northern communities in Canada's territories and the northern areas of provinces like British Columbia, Saskatchewan and Manitoba, are characterized by high rates of child poverty. Further, the inner cities of these same provinces are destinations for dispossessed northern people.

Insidiously, the geographic isolation of the North and the inner city make it relatively easy for mainstream Canadians not to see the hardship of life there. "Out of sight, out of mind" appears to be a social and a political reality in Canada. However, geographical invisibility, as an explanation, is too simplistic. Mainstream society, in fact, seems to justify its indifference with t he following belief: if people are disadvantaged by where they live, they should just move to where they can improve their lives. As Canadians, we have a collectively held, abstract belief that our system of social welfare is in place to help and protect the poor and that poor people choose not to partake of social and economic benefits. Universal health care is there for the taking, we think. Interestingly, though, as I demonstrate in the next chapter, universal health care does not translate into universal health and well-being. Our absolute belief that Canada protects those in need makes us blind or indifferent to children in need within our own borders, especially when those children live in places most Canadians do not visit, including northern regions and inner cities.

Childhood Exploitation and Abuse and Generational Damage

Probably the most fundamental insights for understanding persistent child poverty can be found within the patterns of generational damage. The history of sexual and physical abuse of children and youth in Canada in residential schools for First Nations children, in boarding schools such as the Christian Brothers' school in Newfoundland, and in foster homes during the last century is well-documented and only recently acknowledged as a substantial human tragedy. Accompanying this historical revelation is the growing knowledge about the long-term damages of sexual and physical exploitation of children.

At long last, the physical and mental injury to children and youth that resulted in future generations of wounded and impaired adults has been documented.[8] The Aboriginal Healing Foundation put it succinctly:

> Intergenerational or multi-generational trauma happens when the effects of trauma are not resolved in one generation. When trauma is ignored and there is no support for dealing with it, the trauma will be passed from one generation to the next. What we learn to see as "normal" when we are children, we pass on to our own children. Children who learn that… sexual abuse is "normal," and who have never dealt with the feelings that come from this, may inflict physical and sexual abuse on their own children. The unhealthy ways of behaving that people use to protect themselves can be passed on to children, without them even knowing they are doing so. This is the legacy of physical and sexual abuse in residential schools.[9]

> **Intergenerational Trauma**
>
> Within the generation of peoples that attended the residential schools programs, the suicide rate within the Aboriginal community is the same as everyone else, but in the following generation it's eight times higher, and they're thinking that it's because those kids were taken away from their parents and don't know how to show that affection to their kids.... It's a huge systemic problem that's generations old. (A youth agency worker in Winnipeg)
>
> Source: A. Curran, E. Bowness and E. Comack, *Meeting the Needs of Youth: Perspectives from Youth-serving Agencies* (Winnipeg: Canadian Centre for Policy Alternatives, 2010).

In 2006, the Government of Canada announced the Residential Schools Settlement Agreement, which compensates survivors of sexual and physical abuse. It also established the Truth and Reconciliation Commission to allow survivors of abuse in residential schools to tell their stories and to make certain that those stories, and the hidden history of abuse, are recorded for all time. The overriding principle of reconciliation applies among survivors, their families and communities, and the Canadian community at large. Given the long-term and intergenerational effects of abuse in residential schools on individuals and communities, the healing, too, will be long-term and intergenerational.

Poverty's Outcomes and the Income Gradient

When children live in conditions of poverty, they are at a considerable disadvantage relative to their wealthier counterparts with respect to physical, emotional and cognitive health. Simply put, poor children do not do as well in life as wealthy children. This means that poor children are at relatively high risk of poor health, low success in education, greater contact with the legal system, greater behavioural problems in their formative years and victimization. Probably the most persistent finding in research on the human condition is that well-being in many forms is related to one's socio-economic status, often measured by income, occupational prestige and education. The "income gradient" (sometimes referred to as the socio-economic gradient) is a term used in academic and public policy circles to refer to the relationship between socio-economic well-being and human or personal well-being.

With respect to children, it describes the condition in which poor children are more likely than wealthy children to experience jeopardy in many forms. With respect to health, poorer children will have greater levels of childhood obesity, poorer teeth, poorer nutrition and greater risk of contracting communicable diseases, in large part because wealthy families have the resources to manage both temporary and chronic conditions better than poor families. In education, poor children have lower levels of cognitive skills (including math and vocabulary), poorer social skills and greater behavioural problems. With respect to safety and security, poorer children are at relatively high risk from accidental injury, interpersonal violence and self-inflicted injury. The income gradient idea has become so embedded in our collective cultural beliefs that we associate children in trouble or at risk with poor children, despite the fact that this is not always the case. In short, when politicians, policy makers and others involved in the welfare of children discuss children at risk, they often engage in talk that masks the reality that childhood disadvantage stems primarily from lack of access to a decent standard of living.

Family Support, Lone Parenthood and Children in Poverty

Often ignored in child poverty debates is the reality that children living in poverty is really about "families living in poverty." Most people are fully aware that families need the resources and the time to raise children well. One of our cultural misconceptions, however, is that when children do not do as well as they should, when they are in jeopardy, the parents are at fault. This is the essence of the family values debates that have gone on for decades in North America; they are based on the flawed assumption that bad kids come from bad parents and that if certain parents would simply be better guardians and mentors, their kids would be better. Lone parents, especially single mothers, often bear the brunt of public condemnation. And, in Canada, a much higher proportion of lone parent families live below the poverty line than any other family type. In 2004, 50 percent of single mothers lived $9000 below the poverty line, compared to 10 percent of all families with children. The proportion of lone parent families characterized by child poverty is dramatically higher than dual parent families for all provinces, although some provinces are better in this regard than others (see Figure 1.3). Prince Edward Island, Alberta, Newfoundland/Labrador and Nova Scotia have the lowest rates of lone parent poverty. Obviously, it is not necessarily provincial wealth that determines child poverty because three traditional "have not" provinces

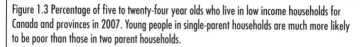

Figure 1.3 Percentage of five to twenty-four year olds who live in low income households for Canada and provinces in 2007. Young people in single-parent households are much more likely to be poor than those in two parent households.

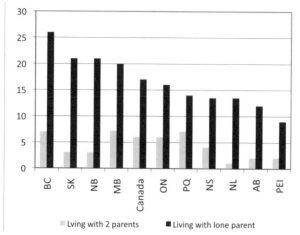

Source: Statistics Canada and the Council of Ministers of Education, *Education Indicators in Canada: Report of the Pan-Canadian Education Indicators Program*, Ottawa, 2009, Table A.3.1.

share the stage with Alberta, Canada's richest province. British Columbia, a relatively rich province, is by far Canada's worst with respect to both lone and dual parent poverty.

Part of the problem in Canada with respect to child poverty is our society's continuing neglect and condemnation of single parent families. This is all the more perplexing given that, especially in the modern global economy, families most often need at least two breadwinners to survive.

This situation is not the norm in industrialized countries. There are numerous developed countries in which single parent families are not condemned to lives of poverty. Comparative international information shows that some industrialized countries not only have lower rates of child poverty than others but also much lower rates of children living in poverty in single parent families (see Figure 1.4). The U.S., U.K. and Canada have rates of single mother poverty close to or exceeding 50 percent. Scandinavian countries, like Finland and Denmark, on the other hand, have rates under 10 percent.

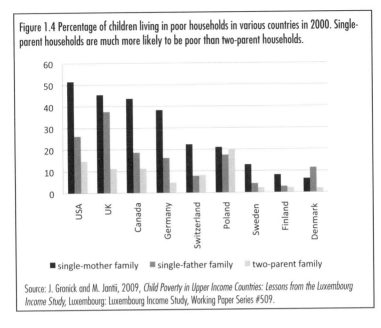

Figure 1.4 Percentage of children living in poor households in various countries in 2000. Single-parent households are much more likely to be poor than two-parent households.

■ single-mother family   ■ single-father family   ▨ two-parent family

Source: J. Gronick and M. Jantii, 2009, *Child Poverty in Upper Income Countries: Lessons from the Luxembourg Income Study,* Luxembourg: Luxembourg Income Study, Working Paper Series #509.

Clearly, North American and Western European countries have a substantially poorer record of providing for single parent families, especially those headed by single mothers, than their Northern European counterparts. Obviously, child poverty and the excessive disadvantages that lone parent families suffer can be reduced dramatically if the right public policy conditions exist. The argument that poverty is a necessary condition of a vibrant economy is difficult to defend, as is the view that single parents produce relatively unsuccessful or troubled kids. The focus for understanding must include issues of social and economic support.

Poor Children, Poor Families

In trying to explain why there are children and youth in Canada who live outside our concern and care, we need to compare ourselves to other equally wealthy countries where child poverty has been reduced to almost negligible levels. We also need to understand that Canadian history is one in which certain groups have gained advantage at the expense of others and that this legacy of discrimination has lasted for generations. We need to remind ourselves that blaming family indifference or laziness for child poverty is unfounded, given that most poor families involve a parent or parents who work in the labour market the equivalent of full-time. Lastly, we need to be clear that poverty has devastating effects on children and their families, effects that violate the *Canadian Charter of Rights and Freedoms* and the *United Nations Convention on the Rights of the Child*.

Chapter 2

FREEDOM FROM ILL HEALTH

In Canada, with our system of universal health care, we assume that children receive the highest forms of primary and secondary health care and that they do so without discrimination. If this is true, young people should be as healthy as other citizens, accounting for the developmental necessities of being young. The fundamental question is whether the inherent right to the best health possible is a reality for Canadian children and youth. This chapter focuses on empirical and anecdotal evidence and examines whether or not our fundamental desire to care for the health of our young is met. If it is unmet, does that happen by omission or commission? What we actually come to know in looking at the health of children is that the income gradient discussed in Chapter 1 holds for health and illness as well as other outcomes of poverty. In other words, health as a condition and health care delivery as public policy vary according to the level of wealth of a child's family.

There is another reality about child and youth health in Canada that needs to be recognized. In our globalized world, child health has become a lucrative international business. A growing portion of the medical health industry is centred on child and youth sickness and disease, especially the mechanisms devoted to identifying new forms of illness and pharmaceutical treatments. Many of the illnesses of young people today really are new: they are maladies that in the past did not exist, or if they did exist, were not considered medical problems. We address this in Chapter 6, which focuses on children and youth as a relatively lucrative consumer market.

The Health Status of Young Canadians

One way of understanding the health of young people in Canada is to look at hospitalization rates (see Figure 2.1). In a country with universal health care, hospitalization should be a relatively good indication of how often young people suffer from illnesses or are hurt.

Our first discovery is that there is a substantial difference in hospitalization across socio-economic groups. Clearly, children from families with low socio-economic status (SES) have greater levels of hospitalization than do their wealthier counterparts. For cities like Halifax and Regina, in fact, the rates for low SES children are double the rates for high SES children. Second, hospitalization rates tell us something about regional health. Regina and Halifax have markedly higher rates of hospitalization than do the other selected cities, most of which are large metropolitan areas. For some reason

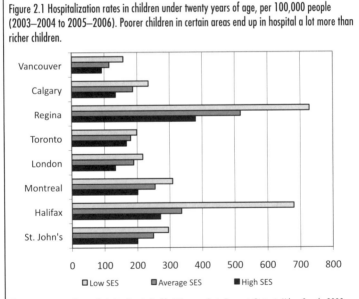

Figure 2.1 Hospitalization rates in children under twenty years of age, per 100,000 people (2003–2004 to 2005–2006). Poorer children in certain areas end up in hospital a lot more than richer children.

Note: SES = income. Source: *Reducing Gaps in Health: A Focus on Socio-Economic Status in Urban Canada*, 2008, Ottawa: Canadian Institute for Health Information/Institut Canadien d'Information sur la Santé, <https://secure.cihi.ca/estore/productSeries.htm?pc=PCC448>.

or other, the large Canadian cities seem to have relatively low rates of hospitalization.

There are three primary reasons why young people end up in the hospital: physical illness, injury and mental health problems. Leaving these reasons for hospitalization unexplored for the time being, I would like to offer two additional bits of information which may help sort out the puzzle of regional disparity in hospitalization rates. The first is that asthma rates for youth almost perfectly parallel hospitalization rates, and Canada has one of the highest rates of asthma in the world. Second, the primary reason boys go to the hospital is for injuries, while for girls it is depression. The rest of the mystery of child and youth hospitalization will unfold in the following discussion of the five dimensions of child and youth health, which, I believe, are the most significant markers for a society and the health of its young.

Infant Mortality

One of the most important indicators of the general health of a society is the rate of infant mortality — the number of deaths of infants under one year of age per 1000 live births. Infant mortality is often used by national and international agencies as a measure of the health of a country. The comparative infant mortality rates of countries throughout the world tell us something about the quality not only of pre- and post-natal health care but also about the general health of fertile mothers. For example, Singapore, Sweden and Japan have among the lowest infant mortality rates (approximately 3 per 1000 live births). The rate for Canada in 2006 was 4.8, which placed us twenty-third among all countries. Our rate was similar to New Zealand, Cuba and the United Kingdom. The United States ranked thirty-third with a rate of 6.3. This ranking placed the U.S. close to the bottom of the industrialized countries, with Canada similarly placed in the lower half of the industrialized countries. The lowest rankings in the world are for countries like Sierra Leone, Angola and Afghanistan, with rates between 150 and 180 deaths per 1000 live births.

For an explanation of the relatively poor ranking of the United States, we need to look at the levels of poverty, especially in isolated rural and inner city areas. The U.S. does not have universal health care, and a substantial portion of its population, primarily the poor and working class, does not have access to health care, especially pre-natal care. Canada's relatively low ranking among industrialized countries is more puzzling. We do, like the United States, have pockets of isolated poverty, especially in the North, where access to adequate health care is not always guaranteed. And we also have conditions of inner city poverty, where people do have access to health care but do not always have adequate living conditions. Poverty does threaten well-being, and certainly maternal health and pre- and post-natal health are in jeopardy under conditions of privation. Although Canada generally ranks near the top of preferred countries in which to live in polls conducted by the United Nations, infant mortality rates have increased steadily since 1960. Canada's rank in terms of the prevention of infant mortality dropped from sixth in the world in 1990 to twenty-third in 2006.

Interprovincial variations in infant mortality help us understand something about regional variations in health in Canada (see Figure 2.2). Clearly, there are variations in population health — as indicated by infant mortality rates — across Canada. In general, central Canada, the Maritime Provinces and British Columbia have rates lower than the national average. At the opposite extreme are Nunavut, Newfoundland/Labrador and Manitoba,

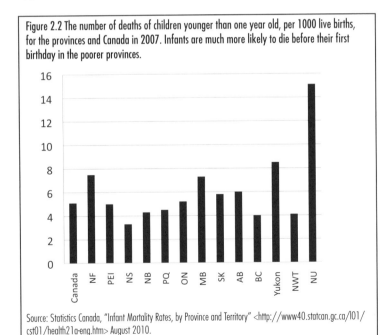

Figure 2.2 The number of deaths of children younger than one year old, per 1000 live births, for the provinces and Canada in 2007. Infants are much more likely to die before their first birthday in the poorer provinces.

Source: Statistics Canada, "Infant Mortality Rates, by Province and Territory" <http://www40.statcan.gc.ca/l01/cst01/health21a-eng.htm> August 2010.

A Young Native Mom Who Just Wants a Decent Home

Lindsay Meekis could not be further removed from the G8 or G20 summits or what they stand for. She is standing on top of a muddy hill at Ghost Point in Sandy Lake First Nations, 600 kilometres northwest of Thunder Bay and deep in the boreal forest. When asked if she feels connected to the $1.1-billion global meetings being hosted by Prime Minister Stephen Harper in Huntsville and Toronto, she flatly answers, "No." She has never heard of either summit.

"Living up north, where we are, nobody really understands how we live," says Meekis. While Canada has consistently ranked as one of the 10 best countries in the world to live, on reserves that number sinks to 63. "They don't know. They haven't been here."

Sandy Lake is a remote, fly-in settlement near the Manitoba border. Meekis, 25, has lived in this Oji-Cree community of 2,700 all of her life.... She is married, a mother and part of the youth council. As an aboriginal woman living in Canada, statistically speaking Meekis faces an uphill climb in life. Aboriginal girls face more gender discrimination than their non-aboriginal counterparts. With a lack of proper health care on many reserves, young women have less access to birth control, medical help during pregnancy and pediatric attention for their babies. Unlike many non-aboriginals, aboriginal women tend not to delay child-bearing until their 30s. While teen pregnancy rates have steadily declined throughout Canada, no such drop has been seen with aboriginal teens. Meekis knows many teens who have their kids when they are 16 or 17. She herself has a son who is 6. She contemplates having more children with her partner, but she is unsure. There is much to consider.

The infant mortality rate is 1.5 times higher for native babies than for non-native infants. And on the flip side, women often must travel off reserve to access abortion. I tell Meekis Prime Minister Stephen Harper has pledged to use his power as host of the summits to bolster the health of women and children in the developing world. Meekis considers this point for a moment before offering that if Harper wants to help women and children, he should consider starting in his own country.

She points out when young women have children, they often can't get proper housing. They bunk with others or family, as the wait for lodging can be years. "For myself, I don't have very good housing here," says Meekis. "That is the same with all the other youth in Sandy Lake." The housing that is available on reserves can often be substandard and in desperate need of repair. Tour around Sandy Lake and you'll see some houses missing siding or outer walls, and plastic or cardboard used to replace windows.

According to the Assembly of First Nations, one in four aboriginal adults lives in an overcrowded dwelling, and 5,486 of 88,485 houses on reserves do not have sewage.

However, aboriginal women like Meekis are increasingly taking a leadership role in their communities to get their voices heard and bring about positive change. Meekis works with the Sandy Lake crisis program. "If there is a house fire I would go help out," she says. "If there was a suicide, then we'd get some help." Boredom, poverty and despair can be overwhelming for youth in the North. Nearly 70 per cent of on-reserve Indians will not finish high school. In Sandy Lake, of 600 young people age 18 to 29 living here, only 20 have jobs. The pain of suicide has left its mark on Sandy Lake, as it has on many First Nations communities. A few weeks ago, a young woman took her life by hanging. The suicide rate of aboriginal teens is nearly six times that of non-aboriginals.

"The youth don't have any activities to do," says Meekis. The youth council is trying to change that, but it is difficult without resources or money. "We barely have any equipment to use so we can't play sports. And they can't afford it."

Source: *Toronto Star*, "G20 Girls: Sandy Lake a world away from G8 or G20 summits," Sunday, News section, June 20, 2010, pg. A7, reprinted with permission — Torstar Syndication Services.

all areas of Canada with isolated northern communities and all areas that experience high levels of poverty. In addition, Saskatchewan and Alberta are above the national average; like Manitoba, they have northern areas with high levels of poverty and geographic isolation. The findings lead us to the realization that infant health and the attendant health of the mother are related to geographic and social isolation and to levels of poverty often associated with isolation.

Birth Weight

Birth weight is an important concern in relation to child and youth health for two reasons. First, weight at birth is an important determinant of overall lifetime health. Infants who are underweight at birth have a relatively high risk of developmental problems, including impaired learning, and a high risk of physical ailments, including sight and hearing loss. Second, low birth rate, like infant mortality, is associated with poverty. In Canada, 7 percent of households with incomes under $30,000 have low birth weights compared to 4 percent in households with incomes over $60,000. Low birth weights are most often the result of issues that are connected to poverty and geographic and social isolation, which include the following: very young mothers; poor maternal health and nutrition; smoking, alcohol and drug consumption during pregnancy; and inadequate health care. For example, fetal alcohol syndrome (FAS), or fetal alcohol spectrum disorder (FASD), has become a fundamental concern for child-care practitioners and advocates. FAS/FASD results from maternal alcohol consumption during pregnancy and its effects can include lifelong cognitive and behavioural impairment in children. Kids with any dimension of fetal alcohol syndrome do poorly in life and often struggle in school. It is important to know that the risk factors for maternal substance use during pregnancy are poor socio-economic conditions, paternal drinking and lack of access to healthy food. The reality is that people in extremely perilous socio-economic conditions use substances, most often in attempts to normalize their lives. A substantial body of research has shown that when socio-economic conditions improve, so do the lives of parents and their offspring.

Simply put, low birth weight is directly connected to lack of basic necessities, including adequate nutrition and meaningful work and leisure. As with infant mortality, the highest rates of low birth weight occur in Canada's north, especially in Nunavut and Yukon. For Nunavut, the rates of infant mortality and low birth weight are over three times those for the rest of Canada. In January 2010, the Canadian Medical Association (CMA) published a study that found that in Inuit communities 70 percent of families did not have enough food; two-thirds of parents indicated that at times they ran out of food.[1] As the South encroaches on traditional communities in the North, traditional ways of living are displaced with southern needs and wants. The fundamental problem is that the economic conditions to obtain those needs and wants in a healthy, sustainable way are often absent in the North, which has become an exploited hinterland without long-term socio-economic infrastructure. The CMA study also found, ironically, that one of the manifestations of lack of access to food is obesity, especially in children. When there is a lack of food security, people tend to eat foods that are high in calories and low in food value. Soft drinks are a typical example.

Cut the Western Diet and Get Moving

Raising children on a traditional diet and staying away from "western" food is the answer to decreasing the alarming rate of diabetes in Aboriginal people, said nutritionist and diabetes educator Kevin White. "It's completely the western diet," said White, who is diabetes educator for the Stanton Territorial Health Authority in the Northwest Territories. Excessive amounts of processed foods, carbohydrates and sugar, which are very present in several of North America's favorite feasts are to blame for childhood obesity in Aboriginal teenagers, he said. Diabetes is one of the many health risks that are associated with obesity....

White is convinced that one of the biggest concerns for children is what they are being served in their school cafeteria and vending machines. Hearty stews in replacement of hot dogs and French fries is something he would like to see changed. Between 2005 and 2006, there were more than 24,000 recorded cases of diabetes in children aged one to 19. According to the 2008 Canada's National Diabetes Surveillance System, both girls and boys with diagnosed diabetes in the one to 19 year age group had a 10 to 11 year reduction in life expectancy in 2005 to 2006. A study specifically done in the Northwest Territories revealed that 44 per cent of people's calories came from sugar-filled beverages, such as soda and juices. Drop The Pop Northwest Territories is a campaign that began four years ago to help encourage schools in the province to educate their students on the importance of reducing the consumption of high-glucose drinks.

Source: Isha Thompson, Windspeaker staff writer, "Cut the Western Diet and Get Moving," Aboriginal Multimedia Society, Yellowknife <http://www.ammsa.com/node/7718>.

Childhood Obesity

It has become fairly common knowledge that rates of obesity among the young have increased substantially, especially in the last few decades. In 2004, 26 percent of Canadian children were overweight or obese. Since 1979, the rate of overweight or obese children has doubled and the rate for adolescents has tripled. For First Nations children, the rates are three times the national average, evidence that obesity is linked to marginalization and poverty. Like other forms of risk for children and youth, obesity and being overweight jeopardize the physical and emotional well-being of the young. Obesity at a young age increases risks for physical ailments like diabetes, hypertension, sleep apnea and skeletal problems. It also increases emotional problems, including low self-esteem and depression, which stem from teasing, bullying and other forms of ostracism.

Why has excessive weight become such a problem for modern-day kids? Like many other maladies, weight problems are often associated with social standing. Poor kids are more at risk than wealthier kids; kids in isolated communities, especially in the North and in inner cities are at greater risk than kids who live in mainstream geographic areas. Families in communities that are poor or socially or geographically isolated have relatively poor access to healthy food and to physical activity opportunities. Historical trends in childhood obesity clearly show that the increase in obesity parallels increases in family poverty and community disruption.

The following scenario helps explain the connection between obesity and hardship. In a poor inner city community in a typical Canadian city, families are often stressed by low wages, lack of work and lack of access to reasonably priced grocery store food. Fast food outlets are common, as are "convenience" stores, which sell a good deal of junk food and pop along with high-priced necessities. In a context in which both parents work outside the home to make ends meet, oftentimes in more than one job, time for shopping and preparing food is limited. Fast food is often the only alternative. It is cheap; in the competitive world of fast food, a burger, fries and a soft drink are a few dollars. Plus it is truly fast, involving no preparation. Consumption of fast food also fulfills the desire of young people to be culturally normalized. Advertising has created a world in which going to McDonald's or Burger King or spending money at a mini-mart are as normal as any other aspect of a young person's life. Many fast food establishments even have indoor play parks. The problem, however, is that fast food is unhealthy, high in fat, sugar and calories, low in nutrient value and large in portion size. Despite efforts by the fast food industry to tap into the health-conscious consumer with salad alternatives, the majority of the sales are still for unhealthy food.

Writer Darcy Frey spent several months with the basketball team of Abraham Lincoln High School in New York, the result of which is his important book on American inner city youth culture, *The Last Shot: City Streets, Basketball Dreams*.[2] He describes the day-to-day lives of four high school basketball stars and offers a subtle, but stark treatise on what sports really means, especially for underprivileged kids living in forgotten communities. As we read his book, we get caught up in the glamour and the potential of basketball as the only route to fame and fortune for kids living in poor, inner city neighbourhoods under conditions of extreme hardship. For a while, we forget that what we are really reading is a story of the exploitation of high school sports organizations for the unabashed benefit of wealthy sports enterprises. For this alone, the book is a must read. It is also a must read because it describes communities like those that I describe above in Canada. The projects area of Coney Island is a struggling community with cheap, rundown high rises that are the last resort for the city's poor and immigrant populations. As Frey describes the only hope for kids in these projects, the hope for a college basketball contract, he also chronicles a community in which amenities are virtually non-existent. There are no supermarkets or libraries, only outdoor basketball courts. The only food for purchase is at several fast food franchises. Mothers and fathers have to commute hours to access grocery store food. For people who are either on welfare and caring for children or working at multiple jobs, buying and preparing healthy food are luxuries they cannot afford. Their children, as a consequence, are exposed to high fat, unhealthy food. This story resonates throughout North America. Even in smaller urban areas, like Saskatoon and Regina, the inner city poor have little access to neighbourhood grocery stores but considerable access to fast food. Inner city communities are in a constant struggle to get and keep viable grocery stores, most often unsuccessfully.

While the relationship between childhood weight problems and poverty are fundamentally important, they are somewhat overshadowed by the fact that obesity and being overweight are contemporary problems that kids face across the socio-economic spectrum. To understand this we must look at the changing culture of children and youth in relation to modern consumerism and technology. To begin with, eating out is becoming more and more normative for some of the reasons described above. Moreover, children and youth are constantly exposed to images of fast food; the influence of advertising is astounding. In the United States in 1998, Ronald McDonald was second only to Santa Claus in terms of childhood recognition; studies showed that over 96 percent of North American children recognized Ronald McDonald and more children recognized the golden arches than the Christian cross.[3] The consumption of sugared, carbonated soft drinks has quadrupled in North America in the last forty years, coincident with the rise of fast food franchises. More money is spent on fast food in the United States than on higher education, and Canada is second to the United States in the per capital consumption of fast food. Britain consumes

Food Deserts and Priority Neighbourhoods in Toronto.

The past decade has seen growing concern regarding the state of food security and nutrition in many North American communities. Food security refers to the availability of food in an area and an individual's access to it. While the benefits of a healthy diet on an individual's quality of life and general health are becoming widely recognized, basic access to quality and affordable food remains a challenge for a growing number of communities. Neighbourhoods that do not have access to good quality and affordable food are labelled as "Food Deserts." These neighbourhoods are often considered to be socially-distressed, characterized by low average household incomes. If policy makers wish to improve the health, productivity and general prosperity of communities within their jurisdictions, addressing the existence of food deserts is an important first step forward….

For residents who live in Toronto's inner suburbs and Priority Neighbourhoods, access to good quality and affordable food is a growing challenge. Today, many grocery stores are located either next to new commercial developments in the inner city or alongside large, retail developments in the outer suburbs. As a result, they are often a considerable distance away from those who live in these inner suburbs and Priority Neighbourhoods, making them difficult, time consuming and costly to access without a car. The importance of nearby grocery stores in the inner suburbs and Priority Neighbourhoods is that they provide easy access to a range of healthy food options, including fresh fruits and vegetables, meats, dairy and bread…. Unable to easily access good quality food, those living in many inner suburbs are served instead by an army of corner, convenience and fast food outlets that offer an assortment of unhealthy foods high in fats, sugars and salts.

Source: "Food Deserts and Priority Neighbourhoods in Toronto," Martin Prosperity Insights, The Rothman School of Management, University of Toronto, June 15, 2010.

more fast food than any other European nation and it has the highest rate of childhood obesity in Europe. Fast food has invaded China and Japan in the last few decades: in China the proportion of overweight teenagers has more than tripled in a decade and a half, and this has coincided with the rapid introduction of fast food outlets. In Japan, during the 1980s the sale of fast food more than doubled, as did the rate of overweight children. This occurred over thirty years ago before fast food was so ubiquitous. The fast food industry has incredible advertising power, which has literally changed the diets of children and youth (and their families) throughout the world.

Another important element of the child weight issue has to do with the changing lifestyles of children and youth. The world of young people is now characterized primarily by being connected electronically for a large part of the day. In January 2010, Pulitzer Prize winning education writer for the *New York Times*, Tamar Lewin, presented the unsettling reality of the day-to-day lives of children and adults.[4] Essentially, young people spend the majority of their waking hours outside of school using some form of physically passive technology, including television, computers, smart phones and other electronic devices. The Kaiser Family Foundation tells us in a new study that eight to eighteen year olds spend 7.5 hours a day with such devices, and because many young people multitask, they experience the equivalent of eleven hours of media exposure.[5] The Kaiser study further found that two-thirds of infants and toddlers in North America watch a screen an average of two hours a day, that kids under six watch an average of two hours of television or videos, and that eight to eighteen year olds spend on average four hours a day in front of the television, in addition to other electronic viewing. This already shocking time use may actually be on the increase as technology becomes more sophisticated.

The implications for young people are mixed. Clearly, their access to knowledge and their ability to communicate with peers and others has advanced dramatically, especially as schools are forced to adopt the technology that young people now consider fundamental to their well-being. Ironically, however, the heaviest users, as the Kaiser study discovered, had relatively poor grades. The other consideration is that the time spent on computers or in front of the television is sedentary time. These large numbers of sedentary daytime hours, coupled with the relatively sedentary nature of education, mean that the young are not physically active. Further, as they spend such long hours in front of screens, they are bombarded with advertising that further inculcates a fast food, consumerist culture. In fact, fast food outlets are in the process of setting up wireless internet capabilities for their customers. Starbuck's has been doing this for several years with great success in establishing young people as target customers. These outlets know full well that the young market is drawn in, in part, by online access.

Emotional Health

Emerging conventional thought has it that the e-world not only creates sedentary young people but that it also creates levels of collective and individual anxiety that are precursors to mental health problems in the young. Constant exposure to electronic viewing contributes to anxiety and behavioural disruption. Many clinical studies concur that over-viewing of television causes increased anxiety in children of all ages, that it increases levels of fear, especially among younger viewers, and that it dulls the desire to be with family and friends. Furthermore, the constant exposure to a vicarious world reinforces gender and racial stereotypes that often frame television presentations. Lastly, an often overlooked, somewhat intangible effect has been raised in the book *Last Child in the Woods: Saving our Children from Nature Deficit Disorder* by Richard Louv, co-founder of the Child and Nature Network.[6] Louv argues that the more kids are removed from nature, in other words the more they experience their world vicariously, the more fearful they become of nature. Louv's worry is that the electronic generation may lose its understanding of and care for nature. The greater worry, expressed by the American Academy of Pediatrics, is that young people lose their ability to empathize with all forms in the world outside and that they may grow to be inordinately frightened of the world in general. The good news is that there is a growing awareness among educators and child advocates that physical education, even just getting outside, is increasingly important, not only to the overall physical and mental health of children, but also to how well they do in their day-to-day lives in school.

Mental Health

According to a 2009 report by Health Canada, 15 percent of Canadian children and youth are affected by a mental illness at any given time.[7] Further, 18 percent of adolescents report a mental illness. The disorders include anxiety disorder, depression, schizophrenia, bipolar disorder, eating disorders and substance abuse. Anxiety disorder is the most common (6.5 percent of all youth), and contrary to popular sentiment about drugs and kids, substance abuse is the least common (.8 percent of youth). Eighty percent of mental disorders emerge in the early teenage years, and they are the most common illness for adolescents. The consensus is that one in seven children and youth by age nineteen will have a serious mental disorder that will influence their development. An attendant problem is that only one in five young Canadians who need mental health intervention receives help.

This is an extreme problem, especially because so many young people are in such mental distress and because society's reaction is largely medical indifference. In 2007, among the twenty-nine OECD countries, Canada ranked twenty-first in terms of mental well-being among children.[8] One of the reasons for our indifference to the mental health of young people may be the cultural assumption that childhood and adolescence are naturally troubled stages of life and that young people will outgrow their distress. One of the realities of schizophrenia for young people is that although the rates for males and females are about the same, males suffer at an earlier age than females and their symptoms are much more pronounced. Ironically, one of the primary reasons that schizophrenia often goes undetected in young males is that the onset of puberty is associated with many of the disruptive behaviours that are typical of schizophrenia. The "boys will be boys" attitude that surrounds public perceptions of male puberty often stands in the way of help for boys with schizophrenia or other mental disorders.

A second reason for our indifference may be that that young people lack the power to have themselves heard at all levels of intervention. They are rarely involved in public policy and are generally not political actors. The public's expectation is also that they are not experienced enough to know what is happening to them. In addition, at school, their teachers are not trained or equipped to handle mental health concerns; the job of teaching is enough work without the added task and responsibilities of mental health care for children and youth. Although young people spend a good deal of time in school, school is not the place for the detection of emotional, psychological or social problems. The primary mandate of education is to facilitate the acquisition of knowledge. Emotional and behavioural issues in school are often relegated to a paradigm of discipline and punishment rather than of medical care.

Probably one of the best indicators of mental distress among a young population is suicide. It is important to underline that for the most part, suicide rates in Canada are highest for young men between the ages of twenty and twenty-four, but the group with the highest increase in the rate of suicide between 1961 and 1991 was fifteen to nineteen-year-old boys. The same trends are true in the United States, where rates of suicide from 1961–1991 for fifteen to twenty-four-year-olds increased four-fold. In Canada and the United States, the rates of suicide for adults and the elderly decreased over this same time period.[9]

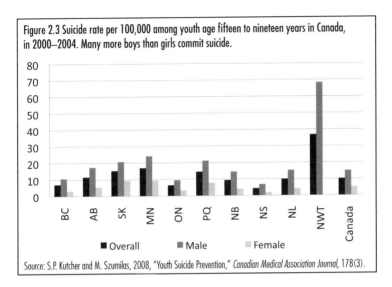

Figure 2.3 Suicide rate per 100,000 among youth age fifteen to nineteen years in Canada, in 2000–2004. Many more boys than girls commit suicide.

Source: S.P. Kutcher and M. Szumilas, 2008, "Youth Suicide Prevention," *Canadian Medical Association Journal*, 178(3).

Figure 2.3 reveals some important issues for Canadian society and the mental health of children and youth. First, it is clear that males are much more prone to suicide than are females. While levels of diagnosed depression are generally higher for girls than boys, boys are far more likely to take their own lives. The culture of being male in modern society is one in which boys are relatively reluctant to seek help for mental health issues, and they are likely to suffer in silence, self-medicate with drugs or alcohol or injure themselves. The most common reason for hospitalization for girls is mental disorder while for boys it is injuries.

Regional variation in rates of suicide is unambiguous. The rates for Nunavut, 577.1 for males, 147 for females and 364.4 overall reveal a suicide epidemic in this part of Canada. The rates for the Northwest Territories are not nearly as high as those for Nunavut, but the territories obviously have high rates of suffering children relative to the other areas of Canada. The provinces of Saskatchewan, Manitoba, Quebec and Alberta have higher rates than the national average. These provinces, like the Northwest Territories and Nunavut, have the following characteristics in common: isolated populations with limited access to mental health care resources; northern economies based on resource extraction and consequent rapid population movements;

and pockets of poverty, especially among First Nations communities. The Canadian Population Health Initiative (CPHA) has determined that suicide rates for Aboriginal youth are five to six times higher than for their non-Aboriginal counterparts.[10] Regional poverty, lack of health care resources, lack of opportunities for young people and the insidious influence of overt and systematic racism all help explain these regional and racial disparities. We can see how community vitality is so important to the mental health of the young in the finding by CPHA that suicide rates for Aboriginal young people are considerably lower in First Nations communities in B.C., with band-controlled schools, community self-government, control over health services, presence of cultural facilities and control over police and fire services. The ability of a community to be sustainable and relevant is obviously very important to the well-being of the young.

Sexual Health

Sexual health is a two-fold issue for youth. First, youth are naturally sexually active, and sexuality and sexual intimacy are, despite denials from certain political sectors of the population, important in the lives of young people. An associated primary health issue is protection from sexually transmitted diseases; in the era of HIV/AIDS, this issue has gained worldwide attention and is probably the focal point of most research on sexually transmitted diseases. Second, sexual health involves how girls and boys relate to one another. Healthy relationships are non-exploitative. Sexual health, then, is really an indication of the health of youth culture. The debates rage on, however, as to whether the demands for abstinence by the adult world are the route to sexual health or if sex education and access to contraception are the answer. Unfortunately, opinions on these matters are often influenced by religious or political beliefs and not the result of good research or practical behavioural strategies.

Ironically, the sexual panic that surrounds young people — that sexual activity is spiraling out of control as are the attendant social maladies like teenage pregnancy, sexually transmitted diseases and overall teenage promiscuity — is quite unfounded. Most current research suggests that young people today are less promiscuous than in the past and are much better at preventing pregnancy than teens a decade ago.[11] It appears that the generation of young people today, from all accounts, shows more restraint with regard to sex than did their parents' generation.

Rates of teen pregnancy tell us something about the sexual habits of adolescents but also something about the use of contraception. It is difficult to determine if teen pregnancy rates are an indication of rates of sexual activity or of the degree of access to contraception and education. Either way, pregnancy is an important indicator of female adolescent health because pregnancy has a dramatic effect on a young woman's life. Obviously pregnancy can have implications for health but also for the ability of a young woman to control her future opportunities; an unwanted pregnancy can curtail education and employment prospects. Whether we like to admit it or not, young women still pay a price for pregnancy while young men who father children may remain relatively unaffected.

Much as with other health issues, teen pregnancy has an obvious geographic aspect. Nunavut, Northwest Territories, Manitoba and Saskatchewan have rates considerably higher than the national average (see Figure 2.4). In addition, Quebec's and Alberta's rates are well above the national average. For the most part, these results parallel the geographic results for suicide and infant mortality. The northern areas in Canada, including northern communities in Quebec, Manitoba, Saskatchewan and Alberta, suffer both social and geographic isolation as well as community and economic disruption. They are, in short, the poorest areas of Canada; health care, health information and the facilities to keep young people healthy and engaged are not as available in the north as in the south. The

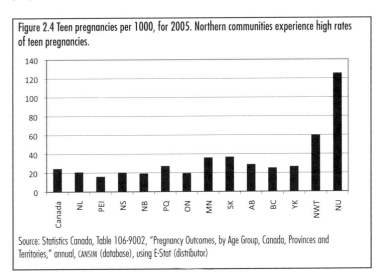

Figure 2.4 Teen pregnancies per 1000, for 2005. Northern communities experience high rates of teen pregnancies.

Source: Statistics Canada, Table 106-9002, "Pregnancy Outcomes, by Age Group, Canada, Provinces and Territories," annual, CANSIM (database), using E-Stat (distributor)

future for youth is bleak in these northern areas. As in most other communities experiencing hardship in the world, teenage pregnancy in Canada's north is closely tied to poverty and lack of community resources. Significantly, the majority of citizens in these socially and economically damaged northern areas are of First Nations ancestry. In the province of Manitoba, for example, the pregnancy rate for Aboriginal girls is three times that for non-Aboriginal girls.

Overall, however, the rate of teen pregnancies has declined steadily in Canada since 1994. This is also true of other industrialized countries, including the United States, which saw rates decline five years earlier. Nonetheless, the U.S. rate remains about double the rate in Canada, and Canada's rate is still over twice the rate for France and Sweden, similar industrialized countries. With respect to actual sexual experience and health, according the Society of Obstetricians and Gynecologists of Canada (2006), the average age for both males and females for the first sexual experience is 16.5, substantially older than the views put forth in popular culture.[12] For sexually active girls, 39 percent in grade nine use the pill, and 54 percent of those in grade eleven do. Ironically, the percentage of both males and females students who report using a condom declined from grade nine to grade eleven.

Another misconception we need to put to right is that the sexual activity of the young has translated into an epidemic of sexually transmitted diseases. Less than 1 percent of all youth report having a sexually transmitted disease. However, since 1992, rates of chlamydia, the most common STD in Canada (which affects young people primarily) have increased by more than 25 percent, an indication that youth are still engaging in unprotected sex to a considerable degree. As with rates of pregnancy, the rates of chlamydia are greatest for First Nations youth — seven times the national average.

In summary, the evidence on safe sex practices for youth in Canada is mixed. Rates of certain types of STDs have increased, indicating reluctance among youth to use condoms or other forms of protected sex. On the other hand, pregnancy rates are declining, evidence that young women at least are using some form of birth control, which may or may not involve safe sex practices. However, maybe the most important issue here is that, despite the public panic surrounding child and youth sexualization, the sexual activity of children and youth continues to be a human rights and public health issue. Many frontline youth workers, including educators, are faced with the difficult on-the-ground-mandate of making sure that children and youth are safe from sexual exploitation and from their own sexual activity, which may place them at risk. The education system and teachers are asked to be a large part of the sexual safety of children. According to the Society of Obstetricians and Gynecologists of Canada, 85 percent of parents want sex education to occur primarily in schools, as does 92 percent of youth.[13]

The need to protect the physical sexuality of the young is compounded by the need to protect their cultural sexuality. One of the reasons why the public panics about teen and child sexuality is that there has been a proliferation of venues for depictions of young people in sexual situations. These popular cultural venues have created a culturally acceptable context in which children and youth become targets of sexual exploitation in rather ordinary, everyday ways. I use the words ordinary and everyday deliberately because that is indeed what the sexualization of young people becomes through vehicles such as the music industry and the internet. Hip hop music, for example, is unapologetic in its misogynist depictions of teenage girls and boys as hyper-sexualized. This particular branch of the music industry has managed to make teenage pornography covertly acceptable in its quest to use sex to sell music. As Craig Watkins poignantly reveals in his book *Hip Hop Matters: Politics, Pop Culture, and the Struggle for the Soul of a Movement*, "hip hop's raging misogyny undermines the movement's progressive claims by glamorizing a culture and sustaining a climate that routinely demeans women at virtually no cost. Significantly, the critics fail to recognize that big media's distribution of such images is a serious health problem, particularly for hip hop's most visible and, arguably, most vulnerable group, black girls."[14]

Sexual Victimization/Children in the Sex Trade

While I discuss issues of sexual victimization of children and youth at other points in the book, the information here focuses directly on the sexual abuse and exploitation of young people, in part, to dispel the myth of the stranger predator. As we will see, sexual abuse and exploitation are mainly at the hands of people victims know and trust or who have been entrusted to care for them. Further, as with most issues of exploitation, there is a connection between marginalization and sexual exploitation.

One of the fundamental considerations in discussing children and youth as victims in the sex trade is that "trade" is a misleading word. The involvement of children and youth in the sex trade is not an issue of the market exchange of money for sexual favours but rather an issue of pedophilia and sexual exploitation. Describing children in the sex trade as prostitutes masks the fact that we are talking about children who are sexually abused by men,

Hundreds of Kids in Sex Trade; Testimony Jolts Inquest; Police Say Hands Tied

Hundreds of vulnerable Winnipeg children, some as young as eight years old, are selling their bodies to adult men for money, drugs and even food and shelter, a provincial inquest was told Monday. But Winnipeg police say there's very little they can do about it. Det.-Sgt. Jeff Coates candidly admitted the most heinous sex offenders — adults who prey on young children — are largely going unpunished because police lack the resources and ability to go after them. Instead, they focus on the easier arrests, such as men targeting adult prostitutes. "It's very frustrating. The worst of these offenders fly under the radar. The worst form of prostitution is allowed to prevail," Coates said....

Coates was called to testify at the inquest of Tracia Owen, a 14-year-old girl who started working the streets in the months before her August 2005 suicide. The teen hung [sic] herself with a rope tied to the overhead door of a garage used by prostitutes behind a Victor Street house. Manitoba's chief medical examiner called for a public inquest last year in an effort to shine a light on the growing problem of youth sexual exploitation and drug use. "We need to tell the public about what's happening out there," said Dr. Thambirajah Balachandra. "No one wants to talk about it, but it's a rampant problem and we have to talk about it."

Jane Runner has spent the past 21 years talking to sexually exploited teens and women about their experiences on the street. She offered some sobering statistics to the court on Monday. Runner, who heads programming at New Directions in Winnipeg, said there are "hundreds" of teen and pre-teen girls working the streets, with an even greater number abused by adults behind closed doors. The youngest she has heard of was eight, and the average age is about 13. She told court that 80 per cent of child prostitution occurs in gang houses and "trick pads." Runner estimated that 70 per cent of the girls are aboriginal, more than 70 per cent are wards of Child and Family Services, and more than 80 per cent get involved after running away from their placements. Runner said a majority of the kids in prostitution have already been victims of sexual abuse. Other common precursors include fetal alcohol syndrome and physical abuse at home. "Unfortunately, we're seeing a lot more of the generations, where maybe the mother or the older sister have been previously involved in the sex trade before they get involved," Runner said.

In the case of Tracia Owen, the teen had been placed in the care of

Project Neechiwan by South-East Child and Family Services, but went AWOL before her death. The inquest has heard that the agency moved her 64 times, including returning her to her parents 17 times before her death. Runner said she believes society largely views children such as Owen as "the bad kids," not as victims. "A lot of people don't see this as child abuse," she said. Runner told provincial court Judge John Guy more public education is needed, along with a greater effort in schools to help steer some of these children away from the sex trade at an early age. She echoed the concerns of Winnipeg police and said a more resources are needed.

Source: Mike McIntyre, "Hundreds of Kids in Sex Trade; Testimony Jolts Inquest; Police Say Hands Tied," *Winnipeg Free Press*, February 20, 2007, reprinted with permission from *Winnipeg Free Press* and Mike McIntyre.

who are, most often, married with children. In addition, our society usually deals with this problem as a crime control issue, using the police and the courts to arrest and detain the victims, not the men. Such children need to be protected from sexual predators. A significant body of research has shown that children and youth in the sex trade are not aggressive criminals, but are in extreme physical and emotional health jeopardy. It has been well documented that life in the sex trade for the young exposes them to high substance abuse, self-injurious behaviour and danger from predators. Such kids have inordinately high rates of alcohol and drug abuse as they attempt to mask the pain and trauma of sexual victimization. They also have high rates of suicide, suicide attempts and slashing. The suicide phenomenon needs no explanation other than that kids escape a terrible life through death. Slashing or other forms of self-injury are typical activities for individuals who live under extremely traumatic circumstances; they attempt to direct their minds to their injuries and away from their life situations. Lastly, the likelihood of a young person involved in the sex trade being physically and violently sexually abused is much higher than for other kids. And, of course, the abuse happens primarily at the hands of men, who are most often larger and stronger.

This discussion about children and youth as victims of sexual predators in the sex trade confronts us with a stark moral contradiction. The kids we are discussing generally live on the margins of the society; they are a highly disadvantaged, wounded group who are on the streets because of poverty, racism, broken families and societal indifference. They are kids who are identifiable primarily because of poor individual and collective health, and yet society responds through the criminal justice system — rightly so for johns and wrongly so for the child victims.

A second dimension of the sexual predation of the young has to do with sexual molestation of children within social institutions. Chapter 1 describes sexual abuse of children in Aboriginal residential schools and also in so-called Christian schools for all children. The offenders in these predatory contexts were sworn to protect and care for the children under their tutelage. As we have come to know, residential schools destroyed generations of Aboriginal families. Religious organizations continue to be brought to court to defend their clergy against accusations of child sexual and physical abuse. Some abuse was systemic and if not overtly, then certainly covertly condoned by religious bureaucracies. In such institutions the offender and victim know each other. In fact, abductions by strangers, while horrific in contemplation, are quite rare. In the U.S., fewer than a hundred child abductions by strangers occur per year, and in Canada, stranger abduction occurs in only .1 percent of all abduction cases. While the concerted public policy campaign in North

---

Molester Usually Someone a Child Knows, Expert Warns

The former police commander Robert Kenary began his presentation with a bold message projected on a large screen: "Stranger danger is not the main threat to your child," it said in large black letters. "It's the stranger you know." In a program for parents and child-care workers designed to prevent sexual abuse before it occurs, Mr. Kenary, a retired 33-year officer, quickly shatters many long-held myths about those committing sexual assaults against children. He brings with him statistics, examples of cases and research from law enforcement officials and psychiatrists.

Don't worry that some creepy stranger will jump out from behind a tree with a bag of candy, he told the foster parents who had been brought together for the program by the state's Department of Children and Families. Don't bank on checking the state's comprehensive sexual offender registry to see if the neighborhood is safe either. In reality, the offenders are almost never strangers; in about 99 percent of the cases, the child knows the suspect well or is related to him, Mr. Kenary said. Moreover, despite every parent's fear of stranger danger, fewer than 100 abductions by strangers are reported across the country every year.

Source: Tracy Gordon Fox, "Molester Usually Someone a Child Knows, Expert Warns," *New York Times*, January 16, 2000.

America to "street proof" kids is laudable and important, the reality is that "stranger danger" pales in comparison to danger from intimates. Ironically, programs to protect children from people close to them are not nearly as well-developed as are the street-proof programs.

One last issue regarding sexual exploitation of children and youth that warrants discussion involves the potential for sexual exploitation via the internet. Obviously, the e-world has changed the way we interact with one another, and young people are especially adept at e-socializing. And, in many ways, social networking has allowed young people the opportunity to interact with one another and form social groups unlike at any other time in history. The dark side of this new e-world is that the potential for sexual exploitation has grown with the technology. Interestingly, we have done a fairly commendable job of protecting children and youth from e-predators because of the diligence shown by police forces in detecting online pedophiles and because of the blocking technology embedded in search engines. However, the danger of e-xploitation exists. In an article entitled "The New Sexual Exploitation," Lisa Tremblay discusses the reality of internet sexual exploitation, including the sharing of explicit and personal images through cell phones and computers. As she argues, what makes these types of cyber-activity especially troubling is that because the activity does not include intercourse, young people do not view it as sexual or as exploitative.[15]

Health and Wealth

The information in this chapter shows the disparities not only of health but of social and economic privilege. Clearly, there is a rupture in our country between the overall health of the privileged and the health of those living in hardship. The stories and examples of health jeopardy described herein are really stories of poverty and marginalization and are an indictment of our collective ability to help the poorest children in our society to have safe, secure and meaningful lives. We have universal health care in Canada, but that is clearly not enough to ensure that all kids are safe and healthy. Health and illness are fundamentally social issues that require political solutions. The medical needs that universal health care addresses are only a small part of the struggle for universal health. In many ways, the discussions in this chapter suggest that the solution to disparities in child health should lie within our innate sense that inequality can be very dangerous for some and is a primary threat to a healthy society.

Chapter 3

FREEDOM FROM LEGAL DISCRIMINATION

The Canadian *Charter of Rights and Freedoms* is clear that the legal rights of all citizens are to be protected and that no one should suffer cruel and unusual punishment before the law. Access to legal protection is foundational to Canadian society. Certainly, the *Charter* and the *United Nations Convention on the Rights of the Child* declare that children and youth must be protected from legal discrimination and excessive legal intervention. We need to ask ourselves, then, whether the legal system in Canada, from the courts on down to the police, really does work untiringly to ensure that children do not suffer at the hands of the law or "slip through the cracks" of legal bureaucracy. One way to assess our treatment of children and youth is to compare their legal treatment in Canada to the treatment of young people in other national jurisdictions, including those with lower and higher rates of youth detention. Another way to assess Canada's record is to observe variations within Canada with respect to the treatment of children and youth in the legal system. It is possible that legal discrimination might be a consequence of public policy gone awry and that discrimination is based on a hidden antipathy to young people. An historical picture will help us determine, too, if the way in which Canada has dealt with young people and crime has advanced or degraded our national human rights agenda.

Justice for Canadian Children and Youth: A Historical Development

Our collective idea of what a child or a youth should be like has changed considerably in the last century. Changing perceptions of young people are often based on whether we think youth and children need to be allowed to develop freely under the close protection of the society or family, or treated like every other citizen with equal rights and equal freedoms. As I mentioned in the introduction to this book, the fundamental issue is our ambivalence about whether a child is vulnerable or competent. Interestingly, the currency of each of these cultural beliefs is closely associated with how integral children and youth are to the Canadian economy. The preference in our thinking for one view or another has been the cultural background and the political justification for the particular youth legal system at particular times.

In the nineteenth century, young people, especially teenagers, were rarely in school full-time. Many children and teens were employed in the agricultural sector and the growing industrial sector and were integral to Canada's expanding frontier economy. Children and youth labourers were "imported" from Europe, especially Ireland, which had experienced a massive potato famine. More and more children and youth occupied public spaces in Canada. When the labour market became saturated, children and youth became low paid competitors for adult jobs. But when young people became unemployed, especially immigrant children without parents, they were perceived as a threat to the order of the society. This, coupled with the growing influence of psychology and psychiatry — which generally saw children and youth as incompletely developed — resulted in the creation of laws to protect young, vulnerable, immature citizens. This was the first time in Canadian history that a separate justice system existed for young people. Up to this time, children and youth were "dumped into the world of adults," where they were treated like any other member of the society. And, of course, when they broke the law, they were punished like adults in adult institutions.

The *Juvenile Delinquents Act* (JDA) of 1908 arose in this economic and social atmosphere with the expressed purpose of protecting children. The Act created a juvenile justice and detention system that was based on social welfare principles. The assumption was that bad kids were the offspring of bad parents and that the state could become the parent (*parens patriae*) if required. The Act did not, in practice, distinguish delinquent children from children in need of protection. As a consequence, young people were assumed not to need the civil liberties that were given by law to their adult counterparts, especially with respect to legal rights in the criminal courts. Judges and welfare workers were given great discretion with regard to delinquents in the hopes that, as children, the courts would treat them like a mother and father would.

The JDA was a tremendous improvement over the harsh treatment that children and youth received in the nineteenth century. However, it resulted in judicial and social welfare discretion that placed underprivileged and marginalized kids at a great disadvantage compared to their higher-class counterparts, who would often be returned to their families upon arrest. Simply put, children and youth from good families were diverted from justice, while children and youth from poor or "bad" families became wards of the juvenile justice administration, often resulting in their prolonged incarceration. Nonetheless, the Act had, at least in principle, the welfare of the child at heart. It had political currency for a long time, almost eighty years, but it started to lose credibility in the 1960s, when legal theory began to focus on the problems associated with a welfare-based legal system. In the country's attempts to be the parent of the delinquent child, the child often became a non-citizen, with no legal recourse and no legal rights, especially no guaranteed access to legal representation. Over the next twenty years, law reformers fought to combine the welfare provisions of the JDA with a new system that would provide for legal rights for children and youth. In 1982, the *Charter of Rights and Freedoms* was entrenched in the Constitution and became another focal point for the legal unfairness of the *Juvenile Delinquents Act*. The *Charter* embedded the rights of children and youth as citizens equal to adults. Under those terms, the JDA was in direct contravention of the *Charter*.

In 1984, the *Young Offenders Act* (YOA) introduced the idea that legal rights for children and youth should be as important as the principle of child protection. The YOA was emphatic in its demand that young people have access to due process and equal treatment under the law while holding on to the fundamental need for society to protect young people. The provisions included mandatory legal counsel and the raising of the minimum age of a young offender from seven to twelve. The Act was created to protect the legal and welfare rights of the young person with the added provisions that demanded youth accountability and parental responsibility. It was tailor made to conform to the *Charter*. It did not, however, sit well with conservative law reformers, most politicians and the media, which sought to discredit the Act for its purported leniency and for ostensibly protecting young offenders at the expense of public security. The media were very much involved in the creation of a popular image of out-of-control young "folk devils."[1]

In its attempts to protect the rights and the anonymity of young offenders, the YOA spawned questions from all political parties about whether youth were figuratively "getting away with murder." Lenient sentences and sentences which diverted young people from the justice system became the focus of contention. The voting public was concerned that violent offenders could receive only a three-year maximum sentence and that youth convicted of murder could not be transferred to the adult system. The public did have rising youth crime rates as ammunition for their claims, but it is extremely important to note that those statistics were primarily a function of changes in police charging practices and reporting patterns. In reality, actual crime commission changed very little. But the partisan and non-partisan attacks on the YOA continued well into the 1997 and 2000 federal elections. Because of the rising tide of opposition to the YOA, it was amended several times over the next ten to fifteen years, which appeased the public's claims that the Act was soft on crime. In 1992 and 1995, Conservative and Liberal governments, respectively, enacted reforms that increased sentence length and provided for easy transfer of violent repeat young offenders to the adult system.

Youth crime, since the inception of the YOA, has become a primary election issue, with all parties adamantly opposed to lenient justice for youth. The panic that the voting public felt and continues to feel about children and youth who offend our sensibilities has been fueled by both partisan politics and by the media, which have, for the last thirty years at least, been on a campaign to show the world the worst, most sensational and criminological images of young people. Clearly, fear drives politics and it also taps into people's desire to stand in judgment of others who are social outsiders — poor, marginalized, minority-group children and youth. Politicians use images of bad kids and panics about kids out of control to build political platforms. The media use images of bad kids to sell television, movies, newspapers and magazines, and they are using sensationalism more and more as time goes on. The result is a public that is more fearful of children and youth than in the past and certainly less willing to tolerate the unique and sometimes inexplicable activities of the young. The ongoing mistrust of young people led to a further reform of the youth justice system in Canada — as we might expect, the safety of the public was the lightning rod that spawned reform. People felt strongly that their lives were increasingly in danger from young people, especially young people who hang around in "gangs." We will discuss this later, but it is important to realize that the assumed increase in danger from young people *never came about*. While youth crime rates do fluctuate, over time they remain relatively constant and in the last few years have actually decreased, as Figure 3.1 clearly shows.

Despite the fact that the Young Offenders Act worked quite well in some jurisdictions — Quebec, for example, used the act to maintain a child protection framework that worked to keep kids out of jail — the public and policy makers expressed a growing lack of confidence in the existing system.

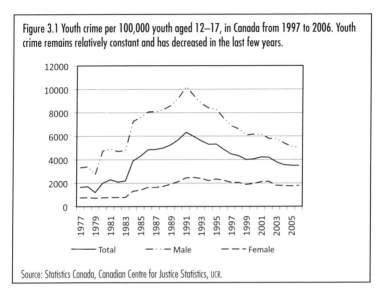

Figure 3.1 Youth crime per 100,000 youth aged 12–17, in Canada from 1997 to 2006. Youth crime remains relatively constant and has decreased in the last few years.

Source: Statistics Canada, Canadian Centre for Justice Statistics, UCR.

Between 1999 and 2003, the public's demand that politicians get tough on youth crime grew. In response, the government felt politically compelled to enact the *Youth Criminal Justice Act* (YCJA). This Act had some important youth-centred provisions devoted to diverting kids from the justice system when possible by providing alternatives to incarceration. These positive provisions, however, were coupled with provisions that were expressly intended to assuage the public in its perception of increasing violent youth crime. Specifically, the Act lowered the age for transfer to the adult system, gave the courts the latitude to send repeat offenders to adult justice and allowed for the publishing of the names of young offenders who had committed serious crimes, something which had been prohibited by previous youth justice reforms.

It is interesting to note that jurisdictions that had a history of dealing with young people with a fundamental child protection/welfare philosophy — like the province of Quebec — were adamantly and officially opposed to the harsh dimensions of the YCJA. And the federal courts declared that certain harsh provisions of the Act violated the *Charter of Rights and Freedoms*. Nonetheless, the YCJA came into effect in 2003 and is the current youth justice framework for Canada. In many ways, the Act is a compromise that strives to balance supportive and preventative programs for children and youth with harsh, law-and-order strategies that give the impression of protecting society from what it perceives as increasingly dangerous kids. Significantly, at the time of enactment in 2003, Canada had one of the highest youth incarceration rates in the world.

There is some evidence that the YCJA worked well from a child protection perspective: the rates of youth incarceration dropped 36 percent from 2003 to 2008. However, as an indication of the value to politicians of a youth crime panic and the currency of youth law reform, the present Conservative government is adamant that the youth justice system is a failure and needs to be replaced with a system that is tough on crime and promotes deterrence. Any actual gains this otherwise more punitive YCJA may have accomplished are being disregarded once again under a backlash mentality which feeds a political will for still more surveillance and punishment of children and youth. Recent research contradicts the logic of this backlash. For example, British researchers have declared Canada's youth justice system under the YCJA to be "a very progressive piece of legislation, one of the most progressive in relation to youth crime passed by a jurisdiction in the English-speaking western world in a number of years."[2]

As we look over the history of youth justice in Canada and various law reforms that have responded primarily to public opinion, we need to be aware that there is a historical reality that stands in contrast to the perennial dislike of the youth justice system and the consequent reforms. For the most part, over time, there has been little increase in serious youth crime; in general, participation rates in all criminal activity are relatively stable. Furthermore, most youth crime is comprised of petty, unthinking acts. The things for which youth are arrested are more closely related to health issues than issues of crime — drug and alcohol use being the most obvious. With respect to public safety, young people primarily commit offences against other young people, those within their peer group, and not the general public, contradicting the fear of adult victimization by the young, which is a constant source of public panic surrounding youth.

There is a final reality about child and youth crime that needs to be discussed but, ironically, the discussions rarely occur in political debates. The fact is that harsh punishment — harsh justice in general — most often leads to more damage to the young person. We now know that jail for young people, especially adult jail, can be very dangerous and also can be a training ground for future criminality. In essence, harsh punishment creates more crime than it "corrects," especially in the long term. It seems so hard for Canadian society, ostensibly one of the most progressive societies in the world, to grasp the idea that tough law and order may create more problems than it solves. Why do we persist on demanding more jails and longer sentences for criminal offenders, especially young offenders?

Canada in Comparison

Canada has had for a long time one of the highest youth incarceration rates in the western world. Our rate of youth incarceration for the year 2000 was higher than that of the United States and, according to Prison Justice Canada, ten to fifteen times that of European countries. Since the inception of the Youth Criminal Justice Act in 2003, our youth incarceration rates have dropped considerably: approximately 35–40 percent between 2003 and 2008. However, our rates are still high in comparison to other countries. Are we to assume that we have more "bad kids" than other nations?

To get a sense of the dramatic disparity in incarceration of youth across developed countries, it is important to realize that several countries, such as Finland, Norway, and Denmark, incarcerate almost no youth — there were seventeen, thirteen and twelve individual youth in custody in 2002,

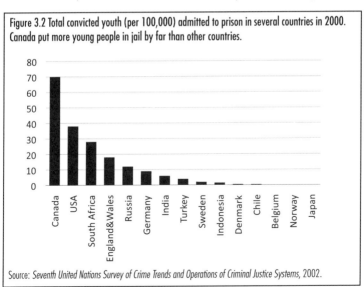

Figure 3.2 Total convicted youth (per 100,000) admitted to prison in several countries in 2000. Canada put more young people in jail by far than other countries.

Source: *Seventh United Nations Survey of Crime Trends and Operations of Criminal Justice Systems,* 2002.

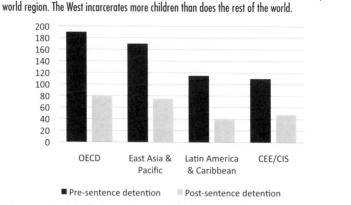

Figure 3.3 Estimated number of children (in 000s) in pre- and post-conviction detention by world region. The West incarcerates more children than does the rest of the world.

■ Pre-sentence detention   ▨ Post-sentence detention

Note: OECD — Organization for Economic Cooperation and Development — North America, European Economic Union, Mexico, Australia, New Zealand, Japan; CEE/CIS — Central and Eastern Europe and the Commonwealth of Independent States — all former Soviet Union states.

Source: P. Moccia and UNICEF, 2009, "Progress for Children: A Report Card on Child Protection," New York: UNICEF <http://www.unicef.org.romania.ProgressforChildren.pdf>

respectively. So, it *is* possible to have a youth justice system based on child protection that treats young people in trouble as people in need of care and consideration without jeopardizing the security of adult citizens. Finland made a concerted decision about forty years ago to abandon punitive justice for kids in favour of alternatives to jail, alternatives that included mediation, community service and community residences for young offenders who are disconnected from their families. The young offender population was reduced 90 percent from the 1960s to the present, and there has been no increase in offending in the last forty to fifty years.

Figure 3.3 shows how the developed world rates relative to less privileged countries in rates of retention. The OECD states, the world's wealthiest countries and least populated countries, have the largest populations of incarcerated youth. The other regions of the world, with higher populations, have lower numbers of incarcerated youth. This rather simplistic pattern tells us a great deal about the structure of the developed world and its relatively punitive orientation toward youth. These highly developed countries have, with the exception of the Scandinavian countries and some others, adopted a criminal justice policy that is unforgiving of children and youth who break the law.

Canada is a relatively homogeneous country; there are not dramatic differences in standard of living from province to province. The exceptions are some northern communities, which historically have been economically oppressed, and some inner city communities, which have been the destination for people who migrate out of poverty-stricken rural and northern communities. With this similarity we would assume that children and youth would receive uniform public policy care across the country. However, this is not the case. Saskatchewan, for example, consistently locked up more young offenders than other provincial jurisdictions in Canada. In fact, Saskatchewan, with the exception of small population-based regional jurisdictions like NWT and Nunavut, has one of the highest rates of incarceration of young offenders in the world. And Manitoba is not far behind. The province of Quebec, on the other hand, historically has used jail very little in dealing with children and youth in trouble. These substantial differences in the actual treatment of youth across Canada beg the question: why?

Regional and sometimes stark variations in the number of youth court cases give us an answer. For example, as Figure 3.5 shows, the number of youth court cases in Quebec is the lowest in Canada. For the most part, Quebec

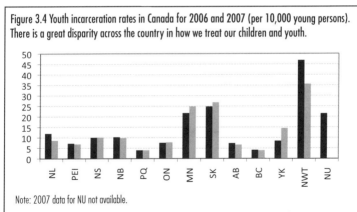

Figure 3.4 Youth incarceration rates in Canada for 2006 and 2007 (per 10,000 young persons). There is a great disparity across the country in how we treat our children and youth.

Note: 2007 data for NU not available.

Source: Statistics Canada, Table 251-0008 — Youth correctional services, average counts of young persons in provincial and territorial correctional services, annual, CANSIM (database), Using E-STAT (distributor). <http://estat. statcan.gc.ca/cgi-win/cnsmcgi.exe?Lang=E&EST-Fi=EStat/English/CII_1- eng.htm>

has done what Finland has done over time. Quebec policy makers have taken it upon themselves to divert young offenders from the formal justice system into the community. Quebec has maintained a "child protection/welfare" philosophy, which is in some ways a holdover from Canada's original *Juvenile Delinquents Act*. The province deals with minor offences outside of the justice system and works to incorporate schools and community services in helping "youth in trouble" to restore their lives. Youth who commit minor offences end up in the court system in Saskatchewan and Manitoba, but they do not in Quebec. As with Finland, Quebec's reluctance to use formal punishment measures for youth has not resulted in higher crime rates. In fact, in Canada, Quebec has one of the lowest rates of violent young offenders.

Interestingly, the Atlantic Provinces have, similar to Quebec, low rates for bringing cases into youth court. These provinces do not have the long-standing formal commitment to diversion that Quebec has, but they do have a more traditional community orientation than many provinces in the West. Newfoundland, for example, is characterized by comparatively high population stability — temporary outmigration when young people seek seasonal labour and little in-migration — which results in tightly knit communities with many intergenerational households. Traditional communities and families

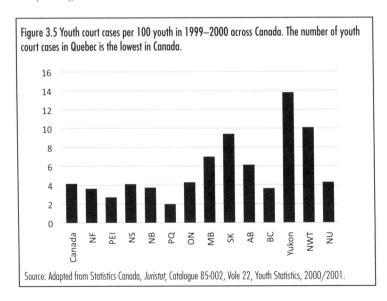

Figure 3.5 Youth court cases per 100 youth in 1999–2000 across Canada. The number of youth court cases in Quebec is the lowest in Canada.

Source: Adapted from Statistics Canada, *Juristat*, Catalogue 85-002, Vole 22, Youth Statistics, 2000/2001.

often deal with miscreant children and youth by themselves without involving the formal justice system. Further, when the justice system is involved, the police and judicial officials are willing to return young offenders to their families and communities, where officials are relatively certain that the young offender will be cared for and her or his violations dealt with.

Another noteworthy case is British Columbia, which has rates of the use of youth court similar to the Atlantic Provinces. Interestingly, the Western provinces show marked differences in the use of youth court despite the fact that the four provinces are relatively similar with respect to economic and social conditions. It seems that the way Canadian jurisdictions deal with young people in trouble is, in part, the result of historical habit. For example, Saskatchewan has gotten into the habit of using the justice system to deal with youth in trouble, and it is difficult to break traditional legal behaviour, especially within a longstanding context of racial discrimination. This also appears to be true for the Northwest Territories and the Yukon. It is, however, less true of Manitoba and Alberta and certainly less true of British Columbia, which has used formal legal control of kids sparingly, despite its recent history as a province with a mobile population and a dynamic socio-economy.

In summary, the use of the courts and detention for young people varies quite dramatically across Canada and is largely dependent on the tradition of the province and territory. In simple terms, some provinces are devoted to keeping kids out of the justice system, some deal with offending kids through traditional family and community systems, and some use justice and punishment. The treatment of children and youth in the justice system in Canada is remarkably diverse, and one might conclude that jurisdictions do not and have not learned from one another.

But, of course, the disparities in the aggressiveness of the youth justice systems across Canada are connected to histories of race relations and racism, histories of immigration and migration, histories of education and residential schools, histories of family support and social services institutions, histories of class relations, and histories of labour. That some provinces engage in aggressive justice as a matter of historical practice is, in fact, more complex than habit; aggressive justice is a consequence of all of those cultural and institutional practices that make up society.

> ### When Justice Means Restoring the Moral Bond of Community
>
> Last year, in a B.C. community, a neighbour checking the house of an elderly woman travelling away from home discovered that the woman's hot tub was being used by several neighbourhood youths. Apprehended by the police, the youths were given the opportunity to meet with the woman and her neighbours in a restorative process in lieu of criminal charges.
>
> The conflict was addressed in a circle consisting of community facilitators, the investigating officer, the youths and two neighbours, and relationships between all parties were built in the process. The neighbours, who had feared retribution from the youths for reporting the incident, have since had their sense of safety restored. The woman is now greeted on friendly terms in the community by the youths and their friends. The youths were restored to a better vision of who they are and are contributing members of their community. Building healthy relationships within a community is one way of "doing" justice and healing interpersonal harms.
>
> Source: Liz Elliott, "Series: Crime and Consequence; [Final Edition]," *The Vancouver Sun*, Vancouver, B.C., May 7, 2003, p. B.6

Justice and Gender

One of the consistent and perplexing realities of children and youth in the justice system is that boys are much more involved in youth crime than girls. While there has been a recent panic about the increasing involvement of girls in crime (associated with rare but high profile cases), in fact, girls offend less than boys. Self-report surveys, like the National Longitudinal Study of Children and Youth, have shown that, on average, 70 percent of girls report no property or violent offending compared to 60 percent of boys who report no property offending and 44 percent of boys who report no violent offending. The research over time indicates that girls are not involved in as much violence as are boys, and when they are, the violence is generally less serious. Boys live in a social world in which they are more likely to become involved in violent offences than girls, and, importantly, their violence is often directed at one another. They also live in a world in which they are more likely than girls to get caught and reported for offending behaviour.

As for the public's concern that girls' behaviour is becoming more violent, although the rates of crime by girls increased somewhat between 1990 and 2000, they have since levelled off. Importantly though, the overall youth crime rate for both boys and girls has diminished somewhat in the last ten years, as has the rate of youth brought to court.

Justice and Race

As in other aspects of the social reality of children and youth, racism is alive and well with respect to the law and punishment. In Canada, the things that put kids at risk, including spending time in custody, vary dramatically by race, especially for youth of First Nations ancestry. In Saskatchewan, Manitoba, the Northwest Territories and Nunavut, the majority of youth in contact with the law and the majority of youth in custody are Aboriginal, in proportions that dramatically outstrip their relative proportions in the population. For example, the landmark Manitoba Aboriginal Justice Inquiry[3] found that 64

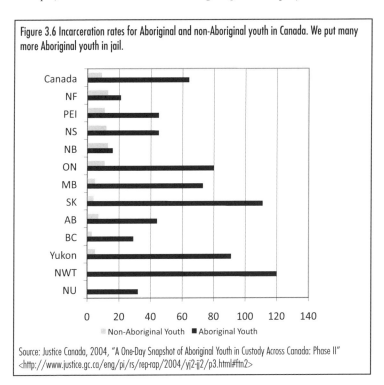

Figure 3.6 Incarceration rates for Aboriginal and non-Aboriginal youth in Canada. We put many more Aboriginal youth in jail.

Source: Justice Canada, 2004, "A One-Day Snapshot of Aboriginal Youth in Custody Across Canada: Phase II" <http://www.justice.gc.ca/eng/pi/rs/rep-rap/2004/yj2-jj2/p3.html#ftn2>

Damaged Children and Broken Spirits

For ten years the federal government of Canada and the Roman Catholic Church imprisoned me. I was terrorized, raped, and beaten. My child's body was not made for violent sexual and physical assaults. I became mentally ill at ten years old. I tried to escape my abuse and torture. Once dogs were used to apprehend me. None of us were a threat to anyone. In that residential school we lived in fear. When we left that residential school, some of us promptly killed ourselves or drowned our sorrows in drugs and alcohol. We went away to hide from our people, being too ashamed to look at them. Some of us died with our shame, therefore leaving our shame to live on in our children and grandchildren.

As an adult, I have been in prison for stealing food and money to eat and feed my family. There is no nice way of stealing food and money to eat. It is done with violence. The irony is that when I was in jail I found it more comfortable than the residential school. The prisons were more humane than residential school. As a child, I needed my parents. Instead, I was subjected to cruel and brutal treatment by nuns and priests whom the government empowered to act in my parents' place.

Source: H. Cote and W. Schissel, "Damaged Children and Broken Spirits: A Residential School Survivor's Story," in Bernard Schissel and Carolyn Brooks (eds.), *Marginality and Condemnation* second edition (Halifax: Fernwood Publishing, 2008).

---

percent of the inmates at the Manitoba Youth Centre were of Aboriginal ancestry, as were 78 percent at the Agassiz Youth Centre. In contrast, the percentage of children and youth who are of first Nations ancestry in Manitoba is approximately 20 percent. Similarly, in Saskatchewan, the Commission on First Nations and Métis Peoples and Justice Reform[4] found that the rates of youth charged in Saskatchewan is more than double the national average, and the majority of these youth are from First Nations.

The over-incarceration of Aboriginal youth in all provinces and areas of Canada is a national disgrace. As the Manitoba Aboriginal Justice Inquiry explained, the high rates of incarceration for First Nations youth occurs in part because relative to their non-Aboriginal counterparts, Aboriginal youth have more charges laid, are less likely to benefit from legal representation, are detained more often and longer, are more likely than their non-Aboriginal counterparts to go to court for a similar offence, are more likely to be sentenced to custody and more likely to serve longer

Meeting the Needs of Youth

"Hunger, poverty, domestic violence, peer violence or bullying, peer pressure for illegal activities, gangs, gang influences, inadequate clothing, inadequate care and attention at home, disadvantages like FAS or learning disabilities... lack of parenting, a lack of direction, and a lack of care."

"People in this area, that we're involved with, are always on the lower end of the scale and have fewer opportunities, and this is because they're living on incomes that you can't do much with.... Depending on how stable the household is, if you're moving a lot, if you're in substandard housing, all of this is going to affect school and their ability to succeed after."

"Our kids have the same dreams that kids in any other part of this city and country have. But they have so many barriers within their own lives to reaching those dreams. For many of them, just basic needs, daily survival, that's where their mind is. It's hard for them to think about their future. It's hard for them to think about their education down the line when all they're thinking about is today."

"Youth struggle with a sense of belonging, and that can manifest itself in many ways. A lot of the time it happens in struggling families, single parent families, or where there are crises in the family because of addictions or other life choices."

"The kids that end up being exploited on the street or drawn into gangs... have those very basic needs of shelter, food, clothing that aren't being met elsewhere."

Source: Amelia Curran, Evan Bowness and Elizabeth Comack, *Meeting the Needs of Youth: Perspectives from Youth-Serving Agencies* (Winnipeg MB: Canadian Centre for Policy Alternatives, 2010).

sentences. In short, there is a systemic bias in the justice system against Aboriginal youth. This type of institutionalized racism is compounded by other forms of institutionalized racism, which impede First Nations youth from obtaining quality education and employment. Embedded racism and discrimination leave not only children and youth but also their communities isolated from mainstream avenues for success. Historical racism, including cultural displacement and cultural genocide within residential schools, has created generations of damaged communities and individuals who have been systematically shunted off to the margins of Canadian society. The historical and contemporary treatment of Aboriginal peoples has created the conditions under which Aboriginal children and youth live in constant jeopardy relative to non-Aboriginal young people

The high incarceration rates for First Nations youth also have to do with the conditions under which many Aboriginal families live in Canada. The Saskatchewan Commission on First Nations and Métis Peoples and Justice Reform asked young Aboriginal people to explain why they are at such high risk of ending up in the criminal justice system.[5] Their voices echoed the findings from social justice research that tell of the devastating effects of unacceptable levels of poverty, high levels of alcohol and substance abuse for them and their families, high levels of violence and abuse, high school dropout rates and deplorable employment opportunities. The conditions of despair described by the Commission and by the young people themselves generate self-destructive delinquent activities.

Youth Justice: Welfare or Security?

One of the only conclusions that we can draw regarding child and youth justice in Canada is that the Canadian state is uncertain about young people. Our continual reform of the youth justice system over time points to a society that cannot decide whether youth justice should be about youth welfare or about the security of the society. And, like so many other jurisdictions, we choose security. Our preparedness to treat violent youth with the harsh punishment that we use for violent adults is testimony to our collective inability to deal with young people outside of a punishment framework. As a society we seem to think that if we punish young offenders enough, we can either stop them from re-offending or at least teach them a lesson. However, international and national comparisons show clearly that harsh law and order is not the only way, and certainly not the most effective way, of providing justice and accountability for the young.

Chapter 4

FREEDOM FROM LABOUR DISCRIMINATION

Recent estimates for child and youth labour in North America suggest that slightly over 50 percent of thirteen to fourteen year olds work during the school year. By age fifteen, about 75 percent work.[1] The surprisingly high number of children and youth who work during their school lives presents another unsettling contradiction for Canadian society. Employment is a focal point in the passage from youth to responsible adulthood and provides the skills, confidence and experience for success later on in life. However, young people can be and often are exploited for their inexperience, their general lack of political power and their willingness to earn "spending money," often for the first time in their lives. Their work is mainly insecure and part-time.

Most Canadians probably assume that youth employment is a safe, necessary apprenticeship for life. In some ways this is true. Young people gain work experience and obviously earn money that, in some instances, contributes to household incomes. However, there is a dark side to the belief that child and youth labour is safe, adequately paid and a learning experience. For the most part, work by children and youth is poorly paid, often below minimum wage, and there are few labour standards to protect youth.[2] It is also relatively dangerous, even seemingly innocuous jobs like fast food preparation and newspaper delivery. Moreover, it is a poor context for apprenticeship because it is made up mostly of unthinking, repetitive routine. And, importantly, what kids are learning from their labour experiences is that adults can exploit them, that doing what you are told is the norm, that because you are young you cannot expect more than you are given, and that quiet resignation is the way to endure — the implanting of labour-rights indifference. The fast food industry is typical of places in which youth work for low wages, are exposed to situations in which burns and lifting injuries

Children and Youth Working in the Fast Food Industry

A selection of responses to "Please describe who you reported the illness or injury to at the workplace, and what happened after you reported it"
I told the shift manager and she told me to get back to work.
I told my boss and so now I'm banned from using the slicer. I reported to my boss, who got me a band aid and then after repeatedly cutting myself she told me not to use the slicer.
The boss, she said be careful next time.
I told them I had burnt myself and they gave me a wet cloth and told me to finish my shift.
To a manager. It was busy so he told me to stop complaining and keep working.
My supervisor, with the head gash we stopped the bleeding and I went back to work.
Duty manager — wrapped dirty tea towel around my wrist.
To the manager and he told me to stay in the staff room for 20 minutes with ice on my arm.
As soon as I got stabbed I rushed to look for assistance however found assistant manager on phone. They continued serving customers while I had to ring for ambulance and police.
My manager said I can go home early but find someone to cover the rest of my shift and the next one.
Reported to my manager and she called my mum, while waiting for my mum had my finger in some ice to stop the bleeding.
Manager — burn was washed with water, I was made to return to work, cut was bleeding for 2 hours, required stitches, but I was made to continue working.

A selection of responses to "Please describe the reasons you resigned or the circumstances that had led to your sacking"
Sacked while sick, off work with medical certificate.
Work colleagues ignored me and wouldn't help me with things I didn't know. I quit as I wasn't comfortable working there.
They took away my shifts and I did not feel safe in my work. I always felt threatened and was afraid of the boss.
I didn't like it. It was heaps of work and being paid $5.60 an hour just isn't worth it. It was also quite slippery in the back so it was dangerous. They expected me to work til 10.30 pm up to 3 nights in a row on

school nights. Sexual harassment, bullying.

Harassment and bullying in the workplace.

When the robbery occurred no phone call or visit in hospital from head office or managers from store to see how I was. Also was sick of been ill treated.

Was told that if I didn't resign I was not going to receive any shifts, so was forced to.

A cook I was friends with suffered 3 degree burns on his arm. I didn't like the way they dealt with it.

Source: Vera Smiljanic, "Fast Food Industry: A Research Study of the Experiences and Problems of Young Workers," (Melbourne, Australia: Job Watch Inc., 2004 <www.job-watch.org.au>).

are common, do mostly repetitive activities that involve little or no intellectual input and can be laid off at a moment's notice, sometimes only because they are ill. The fast food industry is one of the largest, most profitable in existence, and it makes tremendous profits off the backs of very young people who have few labour protections.

Standards for child and youth labourers are strangely uneven across Canada, for example, with variation in the minimum age at which young people may start work. For most provinces, the minimum age is fourteen. In B.C., however, a child of twelve or under may work with provincial permission, and in Alberta, a twelve year old may work up to two hours on a school day and eight hours on weekends. In several other provinces, the fourteen-year age limit is lifted with certain restrictions. In Quebec, there are no minimum age requirements and no limit on hours. The only restriction is that children under fourteen need parental permission. In areas where labour standards for children and youth specify age restrictions, they also allow considerable latitude. When employers manage to circumvent labour restrictions, they still must, by law, ensure that work does not interfere with school and that it is safe.

The law states that employers have a duty of care to protect the welfare of young people in the workplace. Despite that, agriculture seems to be one sector where labour standards are often held in abeyance and where duty of care seems not to be an ethical consideration. In October 2008, Michel Arsenault, a reporter for *Walrus Magazine*, did an interesting and important exposé on child labour in Quebec.[3] He found that child labour is widespread in the province in part because it has been legal for more than a decade.

Child's Play?

Most summer mornings, Luc wakes at five. An hour later, he boards one of the yellow school buses that take him and dozens of other children from the working-class Montreal neighbourhood of Saint-Michel to a strawberry farm somewhere. He doesn't know exactly where it is, doesn't know his employer's name either. But he does know he will pocket $55 at the end of his ten-hour day. He thinks that is good money for a thirteen-year-old; he gives half to his mother and saves the rest to buy his own clothes.

When workers die on the job, inspectors are sent to investigate. Their reports do not reveal the victim's name or age, again in the interest of privacy rights, but those details are found in local newspapers. Clearly, even young adolescents have been killed over the past few years. Maxime Degray, thirteen, had picked corn since dawn in Valleyfield, in western Quebec. It was a late-August Friday, a few days before school was to resume. He fell off a slow-moving trailer loaded with 400 kilograms of corn cobs, and slipped under a wheel. Alexandre Fournier, a fourteen-year-old garbage collector, was waiting for a co-worker alongside a dump truck in Grande-Vallée, in the Gaspé. It was January, already dark on the quiet country highway. A car driver did not see him. The boy was crushed against the truck. Mathieu Desjardins-Levac did odd jobs at a sawmill in Rivière-Rouge, northwest of Montreal. One day, he was sent to the basement to clean a conveyor belt. A co-worker later found his dead body trapped in the machinery. He was sixteen.

Source: Michel Arsenault, "Child's Play: Why Hasn't Quebec Re-Established a Minimum Age for Employment?" *Walrus Magazine*, Oct/Nov. 2008, p. 26–28.

The Quebec situation, along with similar circumstances in other provinces, is indicative of the fact that there seems to be a national ethos that child and youth labour is not a major social problem. But, the realities of kids at work should be a concern for Canadians.

In 2003, British Columbia changed its child labour laws to allow children as young as twelve into the workplace. A report subsequent to this legislation determined that child workplace injuries increased ten-fold and that injuries occurred most often in accommodation and food services, retail, agriculture, food and beverage manufacturing and, unbelievably, construction.

How does one explain the state of children and youth working in Canada? If we observe the international situation, it is clear that despite the

United Nations Declaration on the Rights of the Child in 1989, 250 million children ages five to fifteen worldwide work long hours in hazardous conditions. Most children in the developing world who work do so because they have to contribute to family survival. This is one of the reasons why children and youth work in Canada as well. Arsenault found that in Quebec, many of the children who worked long hours often did so to help support their families. This finding stands in stark contrast to the public perception that young people work for money to spend on trivial consumer items. In Canada child labour is often related to family poverty. The cultural ethos that supports unregulated child and youth labour hearkens back to a time when settling the Canadian wilderness was accompanied by considerable economic and physical hardship — a time when children and youth worked alongside adult family members as an act of family survival.

Sociologist Sandra Rollings-Magnuson has written a compelling book, *Heavy Burden on Small Shoulders: The Labour of Pioneer Children on the Canadian Prairie*, in which she describes turn-of-the-century Western Canada and the importance of child labour to pioneering families.[4] With the demands of making a living and the demands imposed by governments that made ownership of land contingent on a certain level of productivity within a certain time period, children were required to make substantial labour contributions to farm survival. Rollings-Magnusson's book describes a period in which child and youth labour was not only necessary but part of the apprenticeship for life. Because of this, parents and other family members provided close guidance to ensure that child and youth work was not only as safe as possible but also an opportunity to learn valuable life and survival skills. Children and youth often worked alongside their parents and cared for younger siblings when parents were busy. They became skilled in farming and domestic and child-rearing work, skills that prepared them well for adulthood. In that historical context, it is understandable that child and youth labour was considered normal.

Interestingly, we have not relinquished the conviction that children should help out with farming. At present in Alberta, children and adolescents engaged in agricultural work are exempt from labour standards regulating the employment of the young. In fact, in religious/ethnic communities, regulation is non-existent. Moreover, current estimates suggest that 8.7 percent of children (aged nine to eleven) and 29.4 percent of adolescents (aged twelve to fourteen) are engaged in labour outside the home.[5] Also, while labour standards across Canada prohibit adolescent labour that is dangerous or interrupts the formal education of the young person, industries can make application for exceptions to the standards. In Alberta in the last five or more years, these applications have risen dramatically, as has the success of such applications.

In essence, when the economy of a region demands the employment of the young, modern society complies. The difference is, however, that in a past such as that described by Rollings-Magnusson, the work of children and youth was part of the collective family work, was generally non-waged, non-exploitative and certainly skill-developing. In the modern world of child and youth work, it is difficult to make the same claim. Modern agricultural labour is highly industrialized, machine-based, demanding of adult-like skills and dangerous as a consequence.

The modern state has determined that the family is responsible for the safety of its children. The state will intervene only upon complaint and then only in a reactive, case-by-case remedial manner. The problem is that children and youth are generally the only ones in a position to bring a complaint, and they are unlikely to do so or to be listened to. Children and youth often do not know their rights and have much less power than their adult counterparts. They are in a submissive position, not only because they are employees but also because they are children living in an adult world. An example of the violation of the labour rights of the young, violations that seem to occur almost without any kind of public scrutiny or reflection, may be seen in the state of student internships in the United States.

In the United States in 1992, only 9 percent of college graduating students participated in internships; by 2006, 83 percent were involved in internships. Internships have become a fundamental part of college education in the U.S. A recent *New York Times* article based on a report by the Economic Policy Institute reveals that students graduating from high school and post-secondary education are accepting internships with for-profit companies at an escalating rate and that one quarter to one half of them are unpaid.[6] Many companies are requesting and receiving unpaid student interns, in violation of the minimum wage laws in most states. Unpaid internships are available to organizations if they meet several criteria that ensure that the interns are getting experience and education to help their careers; the internships are supposed to be about aiding the student and not the organization. However, most unpaid internships involve menial work with no educative function or mentoring.

In an economic context in which labour opportunities for youth are limited, many companies are using internships for free labour. This practice continues, in part, because students are reluctant to complain for fear of jeopardizing their future job opportunities and because they feel they need positive references from employers as an important component of their resumés. In addition, troubled economic conditions including high unemployment rates create a climate of public fear and are a constant reminder to young people that they have to do this exploitative work to get jobs later. The Economic Policy Institute also points out that not only is there a rapid expansion in unpaid internships, the majority of interns are unprotected by discrimination and harassment statutes.

In Canada, high school and college unpaid internships are also common and are almost universally accepted as a necessary part of educational development. The private, public and non-profit sectors offer expanding opportunities for young people to engage in unpaid internships, often with the potential for future employment. Whether Canadian organizations will follow their U.S. counterparts and use unpaid internships as a form of free labour (without educative mentoring) remains to be seen, but the U.S. example should sound a warning. In both countries, unpaid internships are available to young people who can afford not to be paid. This means that unpaid internships give advantage to youth from already privileged homes, while poorer students cannot afford to seek or accept them. The internship program may, in the end, foster greater disparities between have and have-not families. "If you're a for-profit employer or you want to pursue an internship with a for-profit employer, there aren't going to be many circumstances where you can have an internship and not be paid and still be in compliance with the law," said Nancy J. Leppink, the acting director of the department's wage and hour division.

Labour and the Safety of Young People

While some young people are still involved in agricultural labour, the majority of school-age kids take jobs in the fast food industry and other forms of retailing, job contexts that seem relatively safe. But is modern labour for youth safer than in the past? Is it safer than adult work?

We know that the majority of school-age children and youth are working, and the cumulative evidence shows that, overall, the labour of young people is quite dangerous. The high rates of labour injuries in the Western provinces are, in part, the result of children and youth working on farms with little or no labour standards to ensure their safety. I indicated earlier that agricultural work in the past was relatively safe, partly because of presence of parents and the culture of mentorship. Today, agricultural work is especially dangerous, in

---

The Unpaid Intern

"We've had cases where unpaid interns really were displacing workers and where they weren't being supervised in an educational capacity," said Bob Estabrook, spokesman for Oregon's labor department. His department recently handled complaints involving two individuals at a solar panel company who received $3,350 in back pay after claiming that they were wrongly treated as unpaid interns. Many students said they had held internships that involved non-educational menial work. To be sure, many internships involve some unskilled work, but when the jobs are mostly drudgery, regulators say, it is clearly illegal not to pay interns.

One Ivy League student said she spent an unpaid three-month internship at a magazine packaging and shipping 20 or 40 apparel samples a day back to fashion houses that had provided them for photo shoots. At Little Airplane, a Manhattan children's film company, an N.Y.U. student who hoped to work in animation during her unpaid internship said she was instead assigned to the facilities department and ordered to wipe the door handles each day to minimize the spread of swine flu. Tone Thyne, a senior producer at Little Airplane, said its internships were usually highly educational and often led to good jobs.

Concerned about the effect on their future job prospects, some unpaid interns declined to give their names or to name their employers when they described their experiences in interviews.

Source: Steven Greenhouse, "The Unpaid Intern, Legal or Not," *New York Times*, April 2, 2010, p. 1 <http://www.nytimes.com/2010/04/03/business/03intern.html>.

---

part because machinery is so much more powerful and fast that in the past. Also, though, parental supervision and mentorship are not part of the norm, especially when agricultural survival is so dependent on rapid productivity. There is little time for the protracted teaching of life skills in modern day agricultural production.

Children and youth working in the fast food industry are often the victims of soft tissue injuries, especially burns and scalds.[7] The gender difference in injuries is significant too. The primary workers on farms are boys and young men. In the fast food industry, boys more often than girls do the cooking and grilling, while girls tend to work in the customer area.

That the incidences of child and youth injury are greater than those for adults should give us pause, but there are other factors to consider, too. While work in the fast food industry is relatively dangerous, there is an extremely high rate of turnover of young workers — essentially every worker is an untrained novice. Compounding the problem, establishments are notoriously lax in providing safety training, which, for them, is costly and time consuming. Young people who work in the agriculture and industrial sectors are also novices. Modern day technological agricultural work demands considerable skill and experience, neither of which a young person has. Finally, young people often go to their jobs after school hours; they are at work after a full day of school. Given the developmental needs of a growing young person, a double day is extraordinarily demanding. Young people who are operating machinery or working over a grill under the circumstances of a double day cannot possibly be as mentally or physically alert as the jobs demand.

The following list describes facts regarding child and youth labour injuries:

- The highest rates of child and youth injury are in Saskatchewan, Manitoba and Alberta. Saskatchewan children and youth are about twice as likely to be injured at work compared to their Ontario counterparts.
- Young males are twice as likely to sustain a work related injury compared to young females.
- The jobs that are most dangerous for children and youth workers are in the food service and agricultural sectors.
- In the United States, 54 percent of young workers between the ages of fourteen and seventeen will be injured on the job.
- Children and youth are twice as likely to be injured on the job as adults.
- In North America, between 50 percent and 70 percent of all work related injuries for children and youth involve illegal employment. Illegally employed children and youth are ten times more likely to be injured than their legally employed counterparts.[8]

The fundamental question remains: how have we come to a point at which the labour of children and youth is accepted almost without question, especially given its exploitative and dangerous nature? One response to this question is that we accept child and youth labour because it is a cultural habit. Canadian history is characterized by the view of children and youth as a social problem, and labour has been a longstanding state method for dealing with the "problem."

A Child Labour History of Canada

One of the defining characteristics of Canadian child labour history is that children and youth have been drawn into and forced out of the labour market when the economy requires their inclusion or exclusion. The overall treatment of children and youth has been largely the result of how important children and youth are to the economy, either as cheap labour or as potential, susceptible consumers. Early child labour laws and compulsory schooling were largely efforts to restrict children and youth from the labour market at a time when work was scarce. Their restriction from productive society accompanied a shift in the way we thought about children and youth — from economic assets to economic liabilities. For example, throughout the nineteenth and twentieth centuries, during periods of rapid industrialization, Canada's immigration policy fluctuated based on the need for children and youth to work as field workers and domestic labourers.

Another example concerns the system of residential schools for Aboriginal children. For more than a hundred and fifty years, abuse and oppression were heaped upon these marginalized children and youth with impunity. The child protection/welfare public policy framework in Canada at the time allowed the state and churches to incarcerate Aboriginal children in order to make them "good citizens." The purpose of the residential school system was to assimilate First Nations children into a Euro-Canadian culture and economy. The imposition of a compulsory, and more often than not abusive, system of routine-based education created generations of traumatized Aboriginal children and youth. They were forced to adopt Euro-Canadian values and regimens and forbidden from using their native languages. This left many students unable to fit into their culture of origin and they were always outsiders in the dominant white society.

The forced schooling of Aboriginal children at the end of the nineteenth century was based on a system of alleged apprenticeship that provided free child and youth labour for farms, industries, churches and households. This involuntary servitude extended well into the middle of the twentieth century with the system of "outing," in which Aboriginal children in residential schools were sent to work on farms and in domestic situations as seasonal free labour. In many cases, all able-bodied boys were pulled out of school to help with the local harvest or with wood cutting prior to winter.[9]

Similarly, girls were extracted from school to work in local homes under the pretext of work experience. Schools and government officials believed that domestic labour would not only provide badly needed labour for the community but that it would keep girls "out of trouble" from the sexual advances of peers and prevent girls from compromising school teachers. This racist, sexist and ageist belief system condemned Aboriginal children and youth as sexually volatile and also placed the blame for sexual indiscretion squarely on the shoulders of the children as potential predators, with teachers as potential victims. The attendant presumption was that Aboriginal girls and boys, because of their sexual volatility, could not be trusted to be together. Physical distancing of the genders was based on a longstanding fear and mistrust of Aboriginal children and youth as incompletely socialized and immoral beings. But, in the end, the free labour of Aboriginal children and youth supported agriculture, lumbering, domestic industry and church-based enterprises and was, in essence, a form of slavery.

The system of free child and youth labour under the disguise of mandatory education has historical parallels with other social histories of children in Canada. Well into the twentieth century, the treatment of immigrant Irish children in Canada was no less savage. Youth apprehended by legal authorities were typically white, male immigrant youth who had little schooling, were poorly nurtured and lived primarily on the streets. These "street urchins," or "street arabs," as they were called at the time, came from impoverished urban families who were of first or second generation immigrant backgrounds. Between 1873 and 1909, more than 95,000 children came to Canada from the slums and orphanages of Great Britain. The policy of importing disadvantaged children was the result of a mutual agreement between the governments of Canada and Britain to help solve the "wayward children problem" in Britain. The advantage to Canada was that the policy provided indentured domestic servants for its wealthy families and free labour for its expanding industrial and agricultural sectors and for westward expansion and development. Most of these children lived at the mercy of their adoptive families in Canada, and the historical records show that they were, in general, highly exploited.

Egerton Ryerson and other government-affiliated social reformers who had been influential in the development of residential schools for Aboriginal peoples were of the opinion that Canada was vulnerable to the evils of immigrant children and youth. Ryerson and his colleagues thought that immigrants from the Irish famine "accompanied by disease and death were likely the harbingers of a worse pestilence of social insubordination and disorder."[10] As with the advocates of residential schools for Aboriginal children, educational policy makers such as Ryerson envisioned universal compulsory education as the solution for crime, delinquency and other forms of social unrest committed by marginalized people. The justification for forced compliance was easy: the children and youth who fell prey to the law and ended up in youth and adult institutions were identifiable by their socio-economic and racial backgrounds: they were poor and lived in the inner city and they were recent immigrants or visible minorities. The prejudiced tenor of the times dictated that problems of crime and deviance were easily explained by the "moral incompleteness" of those who were different. It was the same belief system that forced Aboriginal children into a European educational system that essentially incarcerated them in work schools.

Our Exploited Child Labour Force

The labour history above explains much about contemporary Canadian society. The national attitude that allows us to ignore the exploitation of children and youth in the labour force is a remnant of our history. We simply got into the habit of believing that the labour of children and youth is not as important as the labour of adults, a habit that has proven to be very profitable for the industries that rely on kids: the fast food and clothing industries are examples. Whether we like to admit it or not, we do not protect the labour rights of young people as much as we do those of adults. Canadian youth labour history also explains how our educational system became so rigid. It was always based on the assumed necessity of training young people to become workers. And, it was used much more ruthlessly for children and youth in trouble and for children and youth who were different from the mainstream population. The labour history explains how we have essentially lost not only the apprenticeship model for children and youth, but how we have lost the social context in which children and adults occupied the same work world. It is arguable that since the mid-twentieth century, the apprenticeship of young people by adults has been diminishing steadily to a point where it is almost non-existent today. As we moved toward compulsory, formalized schooling, we gradually isolated the child and adult worlds from each other. This isolation extended into the workforce and now young people and adults rarely work in the same labour contexts. Along with that change, we failed to make changes to our labour laws that would protect our large and vulnerable child and youth work force.

Chapter 5

THE RIGHT TO LEARN

We know how important education is to young people's success. Without knowledge and credentials, which education provides, young people will not have access to a respected and comfortable place in society. We also know that universal education is the cornerstone of the democratic state. Against all of these truths, which we assume to be above reproach, are the fiscal and bureaucratic realities of modern education. Education is a public expense and like all public expenses, it is viewed by many as a drain on taxpayers' resources. This ideological position over time has shaped a school system that is business-like in its "production" of students. Furthermore, education appears to give advantage to those already privileged within society.

Educational Success

While education is intended to be equal and adequate for all students, despite their socio-economic circumstances, there is a tendency in societies such as Canada for students from well-off families to do better in school than their less privileged counterparts. Students in academically advanced programs in high school tend to be the daughters and sons of relatively well-educated and financially stable families. Within a geographic context, as well, schools located in higher socio-economic status communities produce students with higher academic success than communities of lower socio-economic status.

Children from low-income families do not do as well as their wealthier counterparts. In general, 10–15 percent fewer low-income children do well compared to children from high income homes. If we look at the relationship between family income and advancing through school grades, four times as many poor kids repeat a grade as do wealthier kids. Similarly, almost twice as many low-income children are in special education programs and in need of tutoring as are high income children. Clearly, low income and poverty are risk factors for academic failure in Canada.

Some students achieve, at least in part, because they have advantages over other students even before school starts. Parents with economic and social power provide their children with advantages that poorer parents cannot. This, however, is not the whole story. It appears, too, that the best schools are located in high socio-economic areas. If we drive through any urban area in Canada, we will often see that the newest, best equipped and nicest looking schools are in relatively wealthy communities. Further, schools in the wealthier areas have reputations, at least among their students and parents, for being "good" schools, "nice" places to be relative to schools in poorer areas. The National Longitudinal Study of Children and Youth, which focused on how parents perceive their children's schools, suggested that this is the case.[1] In that study, parents assessed the overall climate of a school based on their perception of the welcoming nature of the school, the friendliness of the school and whether people enjoy being in the school. The results of their assessments are documented per income level in Figure 5.2.

While school reputations are often based on biases and stereotypes of the communities in which they are situated, schools that are judged to be "better schools" do offer advantages to students that other schools cannot. In fact,

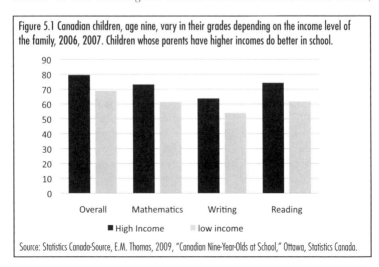

Figure 5.1 Canadian children, age nine, vary in their grades depending on the income level of the family, 2006, 2007. Children whose parents have higher incomes do better in school.

■ High Income   ▪ low income

Source: Statistics Canada-Source, E.M. Thomas, 2009, "Canadian Nine-Year-Olds at School," Ottawa, Statistics Canada.

schools in wealthy areas have high success rates relative to schools in poor areas because they have more to offer, more facilities and more resources.

The advantage that schools in wealthy areas determine for students is compounded by levels of parental participation in school. Wealthier parents spend more time in school and at school activities than do their poorer counterparts. This phenomenon may be the result of social class habit — that

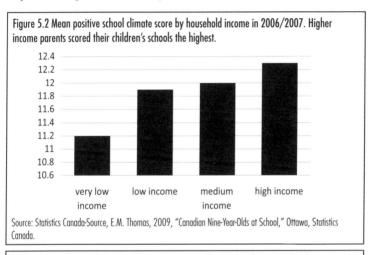

Figure 5.2 Mean positive school climate score by household income in 2006/2007. Higher income parents scored their children's schools the highest.

Source: Statistics Canada-Source, E.M. Thomas, 2009, "Canadian Nine-Year-Olds at School," Ottawa, Statistics Canada.

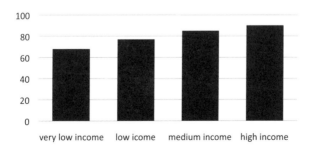

Figure 5.3 Percentage of parents who participate in 4-plus activities by income level. Lower income parents tend to participate less in school.

Source: Statistics Canada-Source, E.M. Thomas, 2009, "Canadian Nine-Year-Olds at School," Ottawa, Statistics Canada.

people with higher education and incomes tend to feel more comfortable in school and feel that school participation is their civic right and duty. More importantly, though, people with low incomes spend a relatively high proportion of their time making ends meet and are not available or in flexible enough jobs to allow them greater participation with their children's schools.

The time that parents spend in school contributes to their children's success in several ways. First, the more time a parent can contribute to the school, the more resources the school has and can acquire. Second, parents' attendance at school is, in part, a political act. Parents who are active in the school can intervene on behalf of their children and can, informally, scrutinize the quality of education their children receive. While this scrutiny may be unwelcome in many ways, it undoubtedly has an influence on educational quality.

Dropping Out

The importance of education in the modern world is confirmed by a trend, at least in the developed world, toward decreasing drop-out rates. Drop-out rates provide a barometer of the importance of education to a society and of the ability of an education system to provide a context in which students feel welcome, motivated and empowered. In Canada, drop-out rates have declined since 1990 (the year we first started measuring drop-outs). In 1990, the drop-out rate was almost 17 percent; in 2009 it was around 10 percent. While this is an encouraging phenomenon, drop-out rates have a distinctly regional and socio-economic character, which tells us something about disparities in Canadian society. For example, drop-out rates are still relatively high in rural areas and small towns, especially in Alberta, Manitoba and Quebec, where one in five students drops out of high school. Further, drop-out rates are higher for boys than girls, and this gap has actually widened in the last twenty years. And, in some of Canada's more disadvantaged communities, drop-out rates are substantially higher than in more privileged communities. Drop-out rates in Aboriginal communities, while declining, are still considerably higher than in non-Aboriginal communities and are declining at a slower rate. In effect, the school completion rate gap between Aboriginal and non-Aboriginal children is widening.

The good news that drop-out rates are declining is buffered by Canada's rank among developing countries. Of twenty-five OECD (Organization for Economic Co-operation and Development) countries, we are in the middle

Aboriginal Youth and School

"[The youth] don't want to be at school, that's what it comes down to, because of various issues, because they're getting bullied in class, because they haven't eaten, lots of our kids don't eat."

"School shouldn't be another place that attacks my sense of self because I can't read, I can't do any of these things. And I don't want people to think I'm stupid so I get out of school or I create an incident. I do something that gets me kicked out."

"There's a fairly high turnover rate of newcomers dropping out of high school, for example…. [I]t seems like they're really struggling to 'fit in' in school, and often, although it's a small minority, some of our youth will get involved in gangs. They just don't have the supports they need to fit in and choose the streets instead of other options…. The gang problem is very inviting with flashy money and all these things. Kids in the gangs speak the same language as them, they appreciate what they do, they offer some kind of a brotherhood, and they find it the most fitting place to belong to."

"[Teachers] are already trying their best by putting in daycare for the young babies and food programs in the morning for these starving kids. There's no social service support for these teachers and they're still demanded to put this curriculum through and teach them math. Well, math is the least of their worries if you're the kid whose starving and just watched Dad beat up Mom last night."

Source: Excerpts from Amelia Curran, Evan Bowness, and Elizabeth Comack, *Meeting the Needs of Youth: Perspectives from Youth-Serving Agencies* (Winnipeg: Canadian Centre for Policy Alternatives, 2010).

of the pack, somewhat better than the U.S, which had a rate of 12.3 percent in 2002, but worse off than a country like Norway, with a drop-out rate of 4.6 percent. Drop-out rates in Eastern Canada have declined much more rapidly than in the West, especially in Alberta, Manitoba and Saskatchewan. For example, in Newfoundland in 1991, the drop-out rate was 20 percent; today it is less than 8 percent. In Alberta in 1991, the rate was around 15, percent compared to 12 percent today. Western Canada is in a modern-day struggle to keep its kids in school.

The disparities above beg the question as to why drop-out rates persist in some contexts and not in others. With respect to gender, female students leave school primarily because of pregnancy. On the other hand, males tend to leave school as a result of two fundamental issues: an overall disaffection with school and/or the desire to work and earn money. In resource-based economies like Alberta, young men can drop out of school and work in the oil industry for substantial wages without much penalty for lack of education. In Alberta's tar sands, for example, the average worker without a high school education can expect to earn in excess of $100,000, significantly more than their teachers in high school.[2] However, such a wage affords only a modest living in an excessively expensive city like Fort McMurray. On the other hand, the Atlantic Provinces have had to struggle to maintain their way of life, even as "have-not" provinces. In fighting to buffer the effects of economic disadvantage, these societies appear to have created a sense of community stability that is important in terms of school success. That their rates of school leaving have declined substantially in the last two decades is a tribute to their focus on community sustainability in the face of economic threat. Michael Corbett, in his 2007 book *Learning to Leave: The Irony of Schooling in Coastal Communities*, argues compellingly that schooling in Maritime rural communities encourages young people to leave in search of a better life.[3] Importantly, however, he illustrates that this only applies to a portion of the young population. Many young people, especially males, stay for reasons that I mentioned above and are less mobile now than decades ago. Schooling is important but less so than the attractions of a local culture and employment.

Gendered drop-out rates also tell us something about the contemporary context of school. The findings of the *Canadian Youth in Transition Survey, 2006–2007* indicate that school is a place where girls tend to flourish more than boys.[4] In the past, collective wisdom and evidence suggested that boys were advantaged in education, partly because of sexist teaching and curricula: male teachers, especially in high school, paid more attention to boys than girls based on an accepted belief that boys would eventually be the primary breadwinners. As a result, scholarship and marks were higher for boys than girls. In the contemporary world, it appears that school has much less appeal for boys than girls; this trend has been occurring for the last thirty to thirty-five years in all industrialized countries. Boys tend to have more trouble with teachers and to be delinquent with respect to attendance and assignments relative to girls. The disaffection that boys feel for school must be, in part, the result of the allure of "oil-sands-like" rewards. As noted above, for girls, the primary reason for leaving school is pregnancy; the 2007 Canadian Labour Force Survey indicated that almost half of female drop-outs had young children and were heading a household.[5] The good news, in this regard, is that

Nutana Collegiate High School Saskatoon, Millie's Place

Saskatoon home economist Millie Reynolds was one of the initiators of Millie's Place, a child-care facility for infants and toddlers of students attending Nutana Collegiate in Saskatoon, where she taught for several years. She was responding to a January 1994 survey which indicated the barriers to teen parents achieving academic success centred around infant/toddler child-care and housing....

Sandi Mair, a public health nurse, and Millie Reynolds, a home economics teacher, contacted people interested in and knowledgeable about teen parenting and The Saskatoon Friends of Students and Kids, Inc. (SAKs), a charitable, non-profit organization was formed in June 1994.

Millie's Place has no shortage of parents seeking spots for their infant or toddler and participating in programs. The spaces have always been filled and a long interest list exists and is being looked into. Of the student parents who used the services in the first year of operation, 7 graduated from high school. Of this group, 6 have continued education in some form. After four and half years of work, the Saskatoon Friends of Students and Kids, Inc. (SAKs) have helped address the needs of some of the student parents attending Nutana. Mike LeClaire, principal, calls the SAKs Parenting Program and Millie's Place the umbrella over many of the service-oriented programs offered within the collegiate.

Source: *Home Economists in the Community.* Homefamily.net <http://www.homefamily.net/index.php/categories/results/home_economists_in_the_community/>

---

school organizations throughout the country are attempting to facilitate the education of young women with children by instituting programs, like school daycare and family counselling, that allow young mothers to attend school.

Problem Kids

It is crucial to discuss the day-to-day reality of school for teachers and students. Much of this reality stems from the issues that I discuss in this chapter, issues that are related to our unwillingness as a society to fund and support education to the degree that we should. When classes are large, when some categories of students are, or at least feel, disadvantaged relative to other students and when families struggle for survival, some students become unmanageable.

Teachers, especially when resources are limited, must somehow manage students who are disruptive, aggressive and often unable or unwilling to conform to the standards of conduct expected in school. Teachers in some schools, especially in schools situated in communities in difficulty, often have to deal with students who are violent towards other students and teachers. Bullying is a reality in most schools, as are physical confrontations between students and staff. Dealing with difficult students is both time consuming and emotionally debilitating for teachers and for students. Our collective policy response has most often been aggressive and punitive — kick the kids out or get the law involved.

It is difficult, in times of acute student aggression and disruption, to remember that bad behaviour often stems from poverty, racism and dysfunctional families and communities, if not abuse. While most teachers do have this insight, the realization does little to help the teacher or administrator on the front lines who is faced with the immediacy of providing safety, security and justice. However, successful, innovative schools do not respond with policies that are rough and aggressive; they build healing into the process of learning. Political support is often weak and temporary for programs that try to provide an alternative paradigm for education, in part, because they are relatively expensive — they often require one-to-one mentorship — and because the results of such programs cannot be gauged in the short term through standardized academic assessments. It is certainly possible that most educators understand the need for holistic-based, long-term, nurturing education, but they are unable to provide it in the continuing climate of education as a fiscal liability. I discuss the fundamental importance of providing a nurturing school environment in the next section.

The School Environment

Most children spend significant amounts of time in school, which is, for the most part, the workday environment for young people, much as the job site is the workday environment for adults. Like adults in the workplace, what young people require in school is a context in which they can have some control, can make a difference, can feel safe and secure, can feel important and can become involved. One of the problems for modern-day education is that school systems are tied to taxation and constantly subject to economic accountability. Education is expensive, at least within an economic paradigm, and quality education is even more expensive. As a result, when public funds are under fiscal scrutiny, class sizes increase, school programs outside of the norm of reading, writing and arithmetic disappear, extra-curricular programs decrease, and teacher wages are frozen. All of these consequences result in a stressed education system and a largely concealed threat to children's well-being. The threat to a child's intellectual well-being occurs directly as a result of reduced educational programs and teacher engagement, and indirectly, of diminishing education infrastructure. School engagement and connectedness are the result largely of several fundamental dimensions: a climate that encourages students to make decisions and to give input into class discussion; smaller school and class sizes; disciplinary policies that are democratic, equitable and not severe; extra-curricular activities; and a diversity of classes that engage a diversity of student interest. In the end, fiscal cutbacks threaten all of these ideals.

School engagement has a long-term impact on a child's well-being.[6] Students who are engaged in school tend to have relatively high levels of self-esteem, high levels of overall health and low levels of anxiety. In addition, they are less exposed to criminal influences and are relatively immune to abusing alcohol, tobacco and other substances, compared to students who are not engaged in school. Every time we cut back on educational programs that diminish the quality of the school and students' opportunities to engage in school activities and the education within, we threaten the well-being of young people. School is that important to child welfare. The chapters of this book analyze the risks to children of poverty and health matters related to poverty. Those matters are underlined when we look at school engagement and health status of young people.

One of the consequences of fiscal constraints on education is a growing parental dissatisfaction with formal education. Parents are increasingly resorting to alternatives to public education to provide their children with what they think are the best educational opportunities possible. More parents in North America, for example, home school their children than ever before. Resources (including chat rooms, online resources, e-lists message boards) and organizations to facilitate home schooling have grown alongside the demand, so that it is relatively easy to be connected to a community of home schooling parents. For some parents who lament the whittling away of public education in the global world, home schooling is a plausible alternative.

Even though dissatisfaction with the existing education system appears to be at the core of the increase in home schooling, for many parents it is a declaration that hides other concerns. The Fraser Institute found in 2008 that parents were also dissatisfied with what they perceived to be a lack of moral/religious education in schools and with the content of what was being taught. They were opting to provide a parochial education in opposition to the secular education in the public school system. Home schooling has become an industry with vast educational resources available for sale on the internet, opportunities to attend conferences to learn about innovations and a new cultural ethos of purchasing the "right kind of education."

In the debates of over home schooling, parent advocate groups defend home schooling as a place of superior moral and intellectual development, an escape from negative peer pressure and a safe learning environment.

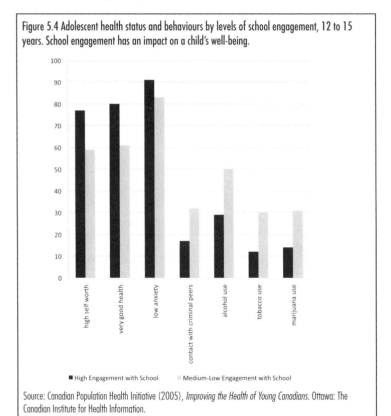

Figure 5.4 Adolescent health status and behaviours by levels of school engagement, 12 to 15 years. School engagement has an impact on a child's well-being.

■ High Engagement with School   ▨ Medium-Low Engagement with School

Source: Canadian Population Health Initiative (2005), *Improving the Health of Young Canadians*. Ottawa: The Canadian Institute for Health Information.

Those who oppose home schooling, including many educational policy makers and providers, argue that home schooling isolates children from their social world and provides inconsistent quality in education. Although home school advocates argue that home schooled children do better on average in standardized high school exams and university admission requirements, there is no sound evidence to suggest that is the case, especially when taking into account the social class of the family and the educational backgrounds of the parents. The reality is that home schooling is not an option for most parents, especially not for poor parents. Home schooling requires time, money and professional networks, of which most families do not have enough.

Education, Television and the E-world

One of the realities that makes home schooling a plausible educational alternative is the enormous power of technology to provide information, access to resources and communities of like-minded people. Technology has grown so rapidly in the last few years that most adults cannot keep up. *Sesame Street* probably created a technological paradigm for the educational development of children in the modern era. Kids who were exposed to *Sesame Street* and other educational programs were believed to have an academic head start. Most parents today would find it inconceivable that their children could become successfully educated without access to a television, a computer and the internet. As we will come to see in the next chapter, Canada adopted a national education strategy in the late 1990s to ensure that all children in all schools would have daily access to the internet, the argument being that the internet would provide badly needed educational resources, even for the most marginalized communities.

What public policy officials and educational experts did not realize is the extent to which young people would themselves become connected to the e-world using their own energy and skills. In fact, adult educators are probably well behind their students in regard to abilities with electronic media. As I mentioned in the introduction to this book, average young North Americans spend the majority of their time outside of school connected electronically in some fashion. Eight to eighteen year olds spend on average 7.5 hours day using a smart phone, computer, television or other electronic devices. And, many of them are multitasking — using more than one device at a time. This rather startling degree of e-use among kids means that they gather much of what they know from the electronic world, either in the form of direct on-screen information or from their friends. If we look at any website devoted to marketing or simply google "kids and marketing," we will find, with amazing consistency, that young people get most of their information about products and services from their e-friends and sometimes from e-strangers. They do this through social networking sites like Facebook and Twitter. Advertisers are, needless to say, scrambling to find a way into the social networking lives of young people, especially given that traditional forms of advertising have a very small impact on the purchasing decisions of the young.

The implications for education are acute. Education systems throughout the world are going to have to restructure the delivery of education to conform to the online abilities and desires of young people. The competition for the attention of young people is going to be tremendous. Schools will not only have to compete for the interest of their students but will also have to rethink the nature of learning. Given the aggression with which children seek out information, schools will have to change to incorporate less teaching and more self learning, because this is what kids are now doing anyway. Another option is to counter e-world learning by creating educational opportunities that take students out of the classroom and into the physical world. What modern students miss is contact with nature and community, and schools may be able to provide contexts for re-learning the physical and social worlds which modern electronic technology have all but obliterated from the lives of the young.

Whatever happens to education, it is clear that the electronic world will be a fundamental source of information and learning for modern young people. And, because technology changes so rapidly, educators will have to be constantly vigilante to understand how children and youth learn, how they communicate and how they form their social worlds. There is a very good argument that more and more social interaction for young people will take place online and that electronic communities will become increasingly important at the expense of face-to-face communities like schools.

A related issue concerns whether educational change in response to changing technology has the potential to democratize learning. Throughout this chapter, we have observed that substantial disparities in education exist in Canada with respect to social class, geography, race and gender. In many ways, how well a child does in school has much less to do with innate intelligence than it does with socio-economic advantage. It remains to be seen whether the influence of information technology has the potential to provide quality education to all children, or whether access to technology will remain a social benefit enjoyed by those who are already advantaged.

Chapter 6

THE RIGHT TO PROTECTION FROM CORPORATE AGGRESSION

Corporate aggression directed at young people may seem somewhat inconsequential relative to the other stresses young people face, but he reality of corporate aggression is profound, not only for those who are exploited, but also for those whose civil and legal rights are denied or, at least, ignored. More importantly, little if any notice attends the concerns that we should all have about children as targets of big business.

The sports, fashion, entertainment and medical supply industries all find markets in young people, markets that are very lucrative and potentially exploitative. Children and youth constitute a major demographic, and the corporate world hungrily maintains its hold on young people as highly susceptible consumers. In many ways, corporations work with medicine, education and sports to initiate young people, and their caregivers, into the realm of consumerism, as part of a popular culture approach to responsible child-rearing. In doing so, the corporate world infuses itself into the lives of the young, sometimes to their benefit, but just as often children and youth suffer as a result.

A notable example of children and youth as targets for corporate marketing involves the ad campaigns for high caffeine, high-sugar "energy" drinks. Beverages like Red Bull and Rockstar contain up to ten times as much caffeine as cola drinks and twice that of coffee. They also contain considerably more caffeine than do caffeine pills, which have health warnings attached to them. According to journalist Carly Weeks, Health Canada says energy drinks pose a very serious health problem for young people.[1] The problem is largely that, despite denials by energy drink companies that

Fast Food Restaurants Target U.S. Kids

Fast food restaurants are stepping up efforts to market themselves and unhealthy food products to children and toddlers with television ads, websites and even their own menus, researchers said Monday. They said efforts by the industry to regulate itself have failed and urged government officials at all levels to declare children a protected group and stop marketing efforts that are fueling child obesity, a serious U.S. health problem. "What we found in the marketing data is a staggering amount of fast-food advertising that starts when children are as young as 2 years old," Jennifer Harris of the Yale University Rudd Center for Food Policy & Obesity in Connecticut told a telephone briefing.

Ms. Harris and colleagues spent a year studying 12 big fast-food chains, analyzed the calories, fat, sugar and sodium in menu items and kids' meal combinations, and studied what children and teens ordered. The report, available at http://www.fastfoodmarketing.org, finds the industry spent more than US$4.2-billion in 2009 on marketing and advertising on television, the internet, social media sites and mobile applications. "Despite pledges to improve their marketing practices, fast food companies seem to be stepping up their efforts to target kids," Ms. Harris said.

Source: Maggie Fox, "Fast Food Restaurants Target U.S. Kids," Reuters, *National Post*, Monday, Nov 8, 2010.

a young audience is their target, they do continuous promotional campaigns through sponsorship of music and sporting events.

Selling Health

Perhaps the not so obvious place to start these discussions is with medicine. Health care and medicine are so important to us in modern society that it is difficult to see, much less criticize, the reality that their provision is the result of careful, calculating business. The health care market is vital, but as with all markets, the greater the net, the greater the business success. Pharmaceutical companies and medical supply companies are some of the largest, most lucrative corporate entities on the planet. And part of their success has to do with providing more and more medical products to children and youth.

The most prominent example of the how children and youth are targets for medical intervention is the modern malady best known as attention deficit disorder (ADD, ADHD). I have already discussed children, health and consumerism in Chapter 2, but here I am referring to the economics of childhood medicine. In fact, discussions about children and youth, health care and corporate medicine really revolve around three complex factors: the desire of parents for the best for their children; the place of education in defining learning problems; and the role the environment plays in childhood maladies.

In wanting the best for their children, parents often participate in their medicalization. Modern education demands that students sit still in class and not be disruptive; a student who is "hyperactive" does not fit into this classroom context. They may not do as well in school work as more attentive students. Active and hyperactive children have relatively short attention spans and cannot sit for long periods. If modern medicine has the tools to help such students stay focused, or at least sit quietly, maybe there is an argument that students benefit from medical intervention. The parents of children who struggle in school understandably want them to succeed, and if a diagnosis of ADD or ADHD leads to medical/pharmaceutical intervention, why not opt for Ritalin or its equivalent, especially if they are convinced it is a safe drug? Many parents decide on medical intervention for their hyperactive children for the very best of reasons. However, in such cases, the presumption is that the child is to blame, or at least that the child's biology is to blame.

There is, however, a convincing counter-argument that active children are not all that abnormal. It is possible that the demands of modern education that a child sit still for hours on end are unreasonable. Most schools now have classes that teach from twenty-five to thirty students per class even though educational research suggests a fifteen-student maximum. Ironically, given the importance we accord to education, public policy managers are resistant to smaller classes, arguing that education would be too expensive if classes were small and one-to-one mentoring were common. Schools are "children's workplaces." But overtaxed teachers and supervisors and limited resources necessarily contribute to schools that are more like warehouses than sites for learning. Like all warehouses, schools necessarily must demand compliant, on-task and mostly quiet "workers." How many children exhibit those characteristics most of the time during the day? And yet if they are not compliant, on-task and quiet, such children — more often than not boys — may be diagnosed with and treated for hyperactivity. Teachers suggest a diagnosis that doctors medicate and parents feel helpless to prevent.

There is a third argument, too, that needs to be made regarding hyperac-

tivity in children as a medical condition. There is a good deal of strong science to suggest that children become excessively active when they are exposed to poor diets, hunger and toxic environments. As mentioned in Chapter 2, allergies to many things have increased dramatically in the last twenty-five years, and young people are exposed to a more toxic environment than in the past. The toxicity can stem from airborne toxins and food additives to excessive sugar or fat in food. And there is growing evidence that the excessive visual stimuli experienced by young people who spend inordinate hours in front of the television, or the computer, or video games contributes to heightened anxiety and lessened attention. Research findings are mixed as to whether the actual content of what is being viewed influences children's behaviour, but the evidence regarding the influence of such media to anxiety and levels of calmness is conclusive.[2] In 2004, the Children's Hospital and Regional Medical Center in Seattle, Washington, for example, produced a study that indicated that every hour children spent in front of a television or computer screen increased by 10 percent the likelihood that they would develop concentration problems and other symptoms of attention deficit disorder by the age of seven. Research since then has shown that being connected, either through the internet or cell or smart phones, creates a psychological addiction that involves instant communication and constant screen interplay. It is easy to see this on a day-to-day basis among young people, who view the cell phone as the most important device they own. Text messaging is a constant reality for many kids; the associated fact is that all of that technologically based interplay stops in the classroom, creating a contradictory and fertile context for anxiety and hyperactivity. Obviously, there are kids who cannot sit still at various times in a classroom, but the cause may not be their pathology. It could easily be their environment, something that can be changed without the direct intervention of medicine.

Selling Food

Eric Schlosser's bestseller *Fast Food Nation* made us aware that the fast food industry flourishes on the low paid, non-secure labour of adolescents. Seventy percent of employees in such industries are under twenty.[3] As I discussed in Chapter 4, the industry depends on short-term, short-work-week youth employment to ensure that it only has to pay low wages, never pays overtime and avoids unionization and on-the-job training, especially safety training. In addition, the fast food industry has openly stated that its target market is primarily children and youth. Despite the health implications of a fast food diet for the young (already discussed in Chapter 2), the industry has directed its marketing almost exclusively to children, so much so that many companies not only feature promotional items for kids — the proverbial toys accompanying kids' meals — but have also created indoor playgrounds for their customers. Richard Louv is a journalist, recipient of the 2008 Audubon Medal, co-founder of the Children and Nature Network in the United States and co-chair (along with Robert Bateman) of Canada's national Children and Nature Alliance. His indispensable study of children and nature entitled *Last Child in the Woods: Saving Our Children from Nature Deficit Disorder* argues that children and their families increasingly look upon nature as dangerous and unpredictable. The open territory of nature is replaced by artificial ecologies, none more obvious than the indoor playgrounds in many fast food establishments.[4] These replacements for nature are constant reminders that the marketing of fast food is directed towards children. Ray Kroc, the creator of McDonald's, knew long ago that that children were his market.

In the quest to sell to children and youth, a host of major companies, including Coca Cola, Pepsi Cola and McDonald's, use schools to market their products. Bottling companies, like Coke and Pepsi, often provide schools with sports scoreboards or educational products, including computers, in exchange for access to school hallways for their vending machines. McDonald's sponsors school events and educational and learning programs to keep its name as background noise in the lives of school children. Its use of philanthropy for advertising, in addition to other promotional campaigns, has been overwhelmingly effective in imprinting on children. In a now famous 2007 study by the School of Medicine at Stanford University, children were significantly more likely to prefer the taste of foods that were wrapped in McDonald's wrappers compared to identical food in a plain wrapper. Interestingly, the study included foods such as carrots and milk, as well as typical fast foods.

For twenty-seven years, Pizza Hut has had a program that gives incentives for students to read. The Book It program provides a gift certificate for kids who reach their monthly reading goals, a certificate that must be redeemed at Pizza Hut for a personal pan pizza. The program has been widely applauded for increasing reading among young people — its proponents argue that it makes teachers' jobs easier by encouraging reading in reluctant students. It even won a citation from President Reagan in 1988. However, current research has shown that, in fact, it has had little influence on reading.[5] Whether it encourages reading or not, Pizza Hut has benefitted substantially in attracting

Kids Say Food from Mcdonald's Just Tastes Better

Anything made by McDonald's tastes better, preschoolers said in a study that demonstrates how advertising can trick the taste buds of young children. Even carrots, milk and apple juice tasted better to the kids when they were wrapped in the Golden Arches packaging.

Youngsters sampled identical McDonald's foods in name-brand and unmarked wrappers. The unmarked foods always lost the taste test. "You see a McDonalds label and kids start salivating," said Diane Levin, a childhood development specialist who campaigns against advertising to kids. She had no role in the research. Levin said it was "the first study I know of that has shown so simply and clearly what's going on with" marketing to "young children."

Study author Dr. Tom Robinson said the kids' perception of taste was "physically altered by the branding." The Stanford University researcher said it was remarkable how children so young were already so influenced by advertising.

But Dr. Victor Strasburger, an author of an American Academy of Pediatrics policy urging limits on marketing to children, said the study shows too little is being done. "It's an amazing study and it's very sad," Strasburger said. "Advertisers have tried to do exactly what this study is talking about — to brand younger and younger children, to instill in them an almost obsessional desire for a particular brand-name product," he said.

Source: Lindsey Tanner, "Anything in a Mcdonald's wrapper tastes better, kids say," Associated Press, *The Seattle Times*, August 6, 2007 <http://seattletimes.nwsource.com/html/nationworld/2003824168_webmcdonalds06.html>.

a new group of young loyal fans. Since the family usually accompanies the child, the restaurant chain increases its revenue, the kids gets a pizza, and reading goals are ostensibly met. In the eyes of the public, everyone wins — but corporations, once again, insinuate themselves into the classroom and into education. Pizza Hut becomes a popular component of raising literate children while it provides junk food to a captive audience.

The importance of this rests not only on the fact that kids are vulnerable to aggressive advertising but also that many of the food products directed primarily at kids are not healthy. A growing consensus among the legal and research communities and health organizations is that the results of such advertising has been the deterioration of the collective health of children and youth. This is evidenced by what has been described by the World Health Organization as a growing epidemic of obesity, not only in the developed world but also in developing countries. Fast food is going global. In China, the consumption of fast food has grown dramatically in the last two decades. McDonald's collaborated with the International Olympic Committee and China television during the 2008 summer Olympics to provide a reality show directed at Chinese children, and its brand name was at the centre of advertising about the Olympics in Beijing. With such efforts, McDonald's has become a major player in the child and youth consumer market in China. Since 1997, China's importation of french fries has increased ten-fold, and the expectation is that its consumption of fast food will increase by almost 50 percent in the next three years. Clearly, Chinese children and youth are the world's most fertile consumer market for fast food. A meteoric rise in adverse health effects has accompanied the meteoric rise in fast food consumption: 10 percent of seven-year-old Chinese children are now obese, and 20 percent are overweight. In 1985, rates for both obesity and abnormal weight were negligible.[6]

Selling Consumerism

While children and youth have been a lucrative consumer market for many years, children's and youth's immersion in the consumer world is substantially greater than ever before.[7] Much of this has to do with exposure to television and the internet. A typical young person's life today is focused on marketed leisure, leisure time that is driven not by their imaginations but acquired in the form of entertainment — primarily electronic. Some have lamented that, as a society, we are experiencing the disappearance of childhood. Such writers blame the concerted and growing marketing and advertising directed at the young for a generation of lost innocence.

Nonetheless, the consumer power of young people is considerable. Two Barbie dolls are sold in the world every second; McDonald's attracts 8 percent of the North American population every day and between 25 and 30 percent of the sales are for Happy Meals (children's' meals); six to twelve year olds visit stores an average of two times per week in North America. And, the more children shop, the more they influence parental shopping decisions. "Influence marketing" is a growing worldwide phenomenon as companies are very aware that adult purchasing decisions are highly influenced by kids. Juliet Shor, in her book entitled *Born to Buy: The Commercialized Child and the*

New Consumer Culture, suggests that Nickelodeon, the number one television show for kids in 2003, had advertisements by Ford Motor Company, Target, Embassy Suites and the Bahamas Ministry of Tourism.[8] Further, car industry estimates suggest that 67 percent of car purchases are influenced by children. Almost all kids' shows on television have associated consumer products attached to them or their brand items attached to fast food companies (often in the form of toys or pictures on cups). As Shor indicates, Pokemon not only has a TV show but also board games, school clothing, backpacks, electronic games and toys at fast food outlets.

One of the questions that arises in discussion about kids in a consumer culture is why they have become so sought after both as actual consumers and as influence consumers. One of the reasons, as I have alluded to before, is that kids are immersed in electronic entertainment and communication. They are, from the point of the view of marketers, easy to reach. Therefore, the world they occupy for a large part of the day is a world in which they are exposed to consumer products. A second, more generic response to the question involves the changes that have accompanied the development of the modern family. Modern two-parent families typically have both parents working outside the home, and single-parent families have become more common. In short, the demands on parents' time are greater than in the past. Marketers have direct access to kids because their parents are not as able as in the past to mediate advertising or to decrease its effect. Kids tend to watch television without their parents; marketers also have direct access to young people through the internet, a world in which their parents are often not as well-versed. In addition, busy parents are less able to spend time preparing meals, with fast food an easy and inexpensive alternative.

The multinational corporations that target children and youth, including food and clothing industries, are characterized by an interesting economic dynamic that presents a third reason for extraordinary levels of marketing to the young. As I mentioned in Chapter 4, children and youth work in fast food and clothing retail businesses, often to earn money to purchase food and clothing. In the past, the money that kids spent on food and clothing often came in the form of "allowances" from parents or from working odd jobs. Now, the equivalent spending money is earned at low wage levels in places like Burger King and Roots. Current research on youth spending habits suggests that a large part of the money is simply given back to the industries from which it was earned as young people purchase fast food and brand name clothing. Essentially, the labour of the young is free. From a marketing point

Children Paid to Plug Junk Food on Facebook and Bebo

Children are being given rewards to promote Fanta, Nintendo and other products to their Facebook friends in a controversial form of stealth marketing. In some cases children as young as seven have been offered the chance to become "mini-marketeers" to plug brands by casually dropping them into postings and conversations on social networking sites.

They can earn the equivalent of £25 a week for their online banter — sometimes promoting things that they may not even like. Among the products being pushed are soft drinks, including Sprite and Dr Pepper, Cheestrings and a Barbie-themed MP3 player. Record labels are also using the marketing technique to promote performers such as Lady Gaga. Multinational companies are using specialist marketing firms to recruit the children after they were banned from setting up fake websites and blogs to target young customers directly....

The marketing agencies advise their young recruits to target different sets of online friends with different brands and coach them to sound "natural and unrehearsed".

Molly, a 12-year-old from Cambridge who did not want to give her full name, has recently applied to a Leeds-based agency called Dubit Insider to promote products through Facebook and Bebo accounts that link her to almost 200 friends. "I heard about it from one of my Facebook friends," she said. "They're going to pay me £25 a week [in gift vouchers] just to say stuff online about sweets and games. They also said they would send me lots of cool samples in the post."

Source: Kate Walsh and Kevin Dowling, "Children Paid to Plug Junk Food on Facebook and Bebo," *Sunday Times*, Feb 14, 2010 <http://technology.timesonline.co.uk/tol/news/tech_and_web/the_web/article7026293.ece>.

of view, it makes good economic sense to target young consumers who have access to labour-derived spending money.

Another important reality in kids' consumer behaviour involves the influence of the education system. In public sector and academic circles, a debate has been going on for years about the real purpose of education. Is the factory-like system of education the best we can afford? Does education have the hidden purpose of training young people to be obedient citizens? Has the education system become part of the economic system whereby the primary function of schools is to teach not only the desire for consumerism but also the rules of consumer conduct? This last question, while controversial, warrants some thought because public school systems are becoming more involved with the private sector in the delivery of education. For example, the for-profit, education industry in the United States currently has revenues larger than the budgets for the military or social services. Companies like Apple, Sony and Microsoft invest in schools through supplying technology and educational software programs. In times of shrinking education budgets, the idea that private corporations can supplement school resources, if only for the sake of advertising, is especially compelling for school boards and administrators. However, corporate involvement in schools presents some fundamental issues that we need to confront, not the least of which is the basic question of whether we want our public education institutions to be sites of corporate advertising.

A second fundamental issue is that when corporations become involved in school funding, they make blatant or subtle overtures toward developing curricula. For example, Future Shop has become involved in funding technology and scholarships in some Toronto schools. Do they have the right, then, to suggest or insist that the software they sell becomes a part of the learning enterprise? These issues become more complicated as access to the world wide web becomes more and more a reality for Canadian schools, even to the extent that access to the internet may soon be considered a civic right.

Interestingly, Canada was the first nation on earth to connect its public schools to the internet. The SchoolNet program was set in motion in the late 1990s to provide not only access to the web for all schools, but also to provide teaching resources and educational news programs to teachers and students. The SchoolNet website was taken offline in 2007 but up to then accessed over 5000 teacher-approved learning resources. This seemingly progressive technological revolution in education also allowed corporate sponsors to display their logos and brands and electronic links to their corporate world. In addition to opportunities to market to school kids, corporations that contributed to the SchoolNet program received tax and in-kind benefits from federal and provincial governments.

Electronic access to schools, then, provides a context in which education becomes, in part, an advertising medium. We are faced with balancing the need to access educational resources for everyone against the expressed right for school children to be immune from corporate marketing, at least within the walls of the school. We are also faced with a more fundamental and probably contestatory question: whether computers and internet access in classrooms motivate students to learn. Many education researchers now question the pedagogical benefits of wiring up schools. On the other hand, the belief from the private-sector-supported, pro-technology camp is that the modern world turns on technology and that computer-based skills are fundamental to success. Children and youth in their non-school lives learn computer skills much more quickly and skillfully than adults. In order to keep up, teachers need constant training, which adds considerably to the already inordinate demands on their time and to school fiscal demands. Many teachers' federations across Canada have, for a long time, expressed the concern that the incorporation of rapidly changing technology into the classroom places demands on teachers that simply cannot be met. In the end, the wiring of education presents a fundamental workload issue for the entire education system.

Perhaps a more important question is whether using technology as a basic educational tool stands in the way of real human apprenticeship. In Chapter 4, I discussed how the world of mentorship for children and youth has changed from a time in which young people worked alongside adults and learned life skills in an interpersonal context. Today, young people's apprenticeship is almost non-existent and technology has something to do with this modern reality. The fact that young people spend so much of their day immersed in technology that is foreign to adults dictates that the world of the child and the world of the adult are separate. Do we want this to happen in schools as well? In theory, we want teachers to be mentors and role models. But in the e-world, mentoring and role modelling are interpersonal practices that are unavailable at worst, and questionable at best.

Finding a Balance

The reason we need to protect young people from the excesses of advertising and marketing is that we want young people to make good choices and to have the freedom to learn by their mistakes. Unfortunately, marketing is so often connected to educational success and to the culture of being a kid that the choices are out of their hands. Technology is the pervasive reality in the lives of the young and in many ways; the electronic world is their world. To succeed social and educationally, young people need to adopt what the consumer culture has to offer. Their social worlds are tied to consumerism; their educational worlds are tied to electronic competency; their educational success is often tied to diagnoses and treatment. It seems that the goal for modern society is to balance the encroaching reality of technology with the need for young people to live well in a social and physical world, a world that seems less relevant than it used to. A balance between the natural world and the electronic world is necessary to control the somewhat unchecked assault on kids as consumers.

Chapter 7

CHILD AND YOUTH RIGHTS

I began this book by offering two contrasting views of children that predominate in Canadian public consciousness: the views of the competent child and the vulnerable child. How we feel about children on the basis of this binary conception often dictates how we view public policy. We want young people, especially the very young, to be protected, knowing full well that their age can place them in jeopardy. The potential for sexual exploitation of children causes us extreme concern and care. At the other extreme, the view of young people as competent often translates to viewing them as aggressive. We want young people to develop into responsible citizens with competency and self-esteem, but we often hear adults express the sentiment that young people are rude, disrespectful and do not "know their place."

In my book, *Still Blaming Children: Youth Conduct and the Politics of Child Hating*, I show that depictions of young people in the news media are inordinately damning, often fraught with images of kids as dangerous, unpredictable and invasive.[1] These portrayals of an immoral kids' culture are, by far, the most common depictions of young people in the news media, and they are often based on commentary that is alarmist. The press often chooses a rare but high profile violent crime committed by a young person, and on the basis of the events of the case, plays to the public's imagination that young people are becoming more dangerous. Reporters use corroboration from officials who are involved with these singular cases to further the public's misperceptions.

The fact is that depictions of children as dangerous to society are not at all in line with the reality of young people in Canada; youth crime rates have been declining for years. Most of the evidence for increasing violence among children and youth is anecdotal and based on the unsubstantiated

A Typical Moral Panic News Story

This is based on selected, sensationalized stories of youth violence against a backdrop of "out of context" statistics. Explanations are given for the decrease in property crime but not for the ostensible increase in violent crime.

Kid Crimes Are on Rise; Violent Incidents Way Up — And Not Just by Gangs

Because they are young offenders, protected and often coddled by the Youth Criminal Justice Act, they routinely escape the media's glare — with only the most sensational of their crimes making it into the headlines. Last Friday, for example, the now-17-year-old killer and ex-boyfriend of 16-year-old Chantele Fetterly of Hamilton was sentenced to two years, four months and 20 days in jail for plunging a kitchen knife into her heart. The Crown initially charged him with second-degree murder, but it was downgraded to manslaughter. The case should have been high profile but, for whatever reason, it wasn't — perhaps because the murder was committed last year in the holiday dead zone between Canada Day and the 4th of July.

Loose Lips

At the tail end of 2005, and early 2006, however, the media in this city was riveted to the story of the two Brampton sisters — both young offenders at the time — who were found guilty of knocking their mother out with booze and pain pills, and then drowning her in a bathtub, a crime with which they might have gotten away if not for loose lips. That story was continually in the headlines. The majority of youth-crime stories, however, were pared down to a few paragraphs on the back pages, primarily because the YCJA handcuffed what the police could release and what the media could report. Truth be known, however, youth crime, in general, is on the rise — with the number of young people accused of homicide reaching its highest point since such data was first collected by Statistics Canada back in 1961.

The latest tabulations by StatsCan, focusing on research compiled in 2006, shows that violent crime among young people aged 12 to 17 has increased 12% in the last decade, and 30% since 1991.

The homicide rate among these same youth, while not in the same league as adults, has nonetheless risen by an astounding 41% since 1997 — with 2006 seeing 84 young people (72 boys and 12 girls) implicated in 54 homicides. Gang involvement, despite the optics of its pervasiveness in big cities like Toronto, was linked nationally to only 22% of those homicides.

Break-Ins Down

If there is any good news coming out of the report tabled by the Canadian Centre for Justice Statistics, it's that youth involvement in property crime has fallen to a third of what it was a decade ago, putting it at is lowest point since 1996. Break-ins are down 47%, minor theft by 33%, and car theft by 41%. These huge drops, though, cannot be directly attributed to wayward youth suddenly deciding to go the straight-and-narrow, but more to the fact that one-third of all Canadian homes now have home-security devices, and that newer cars are increasingly more theft-proof. Still, good news is good news.

Source: Mark Bonokoski, "Kid crimes Are on Rise; Violent Incidents Way Up — And Not Just by Gangs," *Toronto Sun*, Tuesday, July 8, 2008.

perceptions of individual commentators. What is clear from these commentaries, however, is that the press, in trying to sell its stories, and politicians, in trying to get votes through increasing crime control policy, draw upon the public's negative and punitive sentiment, a sentiment that *we* create as citizens of Canada. The fundamental problem is that when we create public policy for kids that is based on a collective emotion of fear and couple it with a parent-like need to protect kids, the resulting public policy often denies the young the rights and privileges due all human beings and assured to adults.

Some people would argue that young people are not allowed to contribute fully to Canadian society and that both kids and society suffer as a consequence. I have explained in this book that much child suffering results from Canadian public policy. Most often, this imposed suffering is not deliberately aimed at the young but is created by adults for their convenience and perceived safety.

If we truly cherish children and know that they are our most valuable resource, why does public policy, either by commission or omission, often fail to care for the young? For example, if the elimination of child poverty (and the attendant problems) is a fundamental Canadian and global priority, why have child poverty rates continued to grow? Most western governments, including Canada, have made repeated declarations that child poverty *will* be eliminated within a certain number of years. In 1989, the Canadian government reached an all-party unanimous decision to eliminate child poverty by

2000, with the unequivocal declaration that the government had the resources to accomplish this goal. In June 2010, Bill C-545 was introduced into the Canadian parliament to eliminate adult and child poverty. Parliament has yet to ratify the bill.

The deadlines come and go, and nothing seems to change for the better. Are we to assume, then, that this is the best we can do, given how our economy works? Or, is there something insidious standing in the way of the pursuit of caring for the young? The rest of the discussions in this chapter are responses to these questions in the form of policy options that might work.

Freedom from Poverty

Chapter 1 was devoted to children and youth in poverty in Canada. Our discussions led us to understand that child poverty is really about family poverty. One of the problems for us is that we find it difficult to address family poverty without laying blame at the doorstep of parents for negligence, laziness, self indulgence and a host of other "sins." The reality is that we can eliminate family poverty. As I mentioned in Chapter 1, some of the Scandinavian countries, countries with much less natural wealth than Canada, have very low rates of family poverty. They choose to spend public money on social justice causes like the elimination of poverty, through guaranteed income and family support programs, and it works, not perfectly, but certainly child poverty is not as epidemic as in North America. These countries make it a priority to raise every family's income to a level at which they can lead lives with dignity, and their child poverty rates are low.

However, it appears that our collective wisdom views such programs as too expensive. This response is somewhat misguided; it is a short-term and entirely fiscal response to human need. We have a moral not a fiscal obligation to eliminate poverty. At any rate, the fiscal argument does not stand up to scrutiny. We now have evidence to show that if we spend money on the elimination of poverty and the creation of just communities, the fiscal payoff does occur in terms of attainable goals such as high educational levels, less ill health and lower rates of crime and incarceration. We could easily provide the basis for better communities both socially and economically. The problem for politicians is that it takes time for the results of social justice programs to come to fruition, and their optics are short-sighted, looking ahead only as far as the next election. The human rights-based goal that every child be free of poverty is not abstract.

Freedom From Ill Health

Much like the drive to eliminate poverty, the goal of getting rid of disparities in health among children and youth is within our reach, especially in the context of universal health care. As we saw in Chapter 2, health status is closely tied to the socio-economic status of families, communities and countries. The problem with the conventional medical approach to health is that we swing into action only after someone becomes ill. If sickness occurs, we have the means to cure, but this is only a small part of health. Preventative (primary) health care is a social and political phenomenon that has very little to do with how good our health facilities are. An additional problem with conventional medical practice (the curative model) is that children and youth become lucrative targets for intervention. The most striking example, discussed in Chapter 6, is the market for pharmaceuticals created by the "invention" of learning disorders and problems with school that we have medicalized into pathological conditions.

Not only do we medicalize social conditions such as low school attainment through a conventional health care model, we also mask social conditions through a personal responsibility model of child behaviour. For example, we perceive the solution to child and youth obesity in Canada to lie in programs that teach kids how to be healthy, to instil in them the habits of a fit person. However laudable such programs are, they run up against a cultural and economic world that fuses fast food with entertainment, education and leisure activity. When we look past the rhetoric of "get healthy programs," we see a young people's world in which fast food sedentary lifestyles are so much a part of their cultural diet and so much a part of education and modern-day entertainment, that to escape the trap of obesity seems impossible without some sort of intervention in the day-to-day lives of kids. Ironically, education is the place where we could make change, but it has to involve a substantial reformation in thinking and practice that would include more physical activity education, more education about food and consumption, more environmental education and more opportunities for leisure time activities inside and outside school, activities that the television and the internet now dominate. The human rights-based goal for all children to be healthy is attainable; it just requires dramatic rethinking of education and leisure.

Freedom from Legal Discrimination

In Chapter 3, we discussed countries in the world that use a punitive legal system only rarely to deal with kids in trouble. Canada incarcerates more kids per capita than any other industrialized country. We should be appalled and ashamed of that first place. In addition, within Canada, great disparities exist in the types of kids who are arrested and who go to jail. Most often, our incarceration rates are associated with race and class. The youth criminal justice system is not consistent, and as history has shown, it has not been very efficient at helping children and youth in trouble with the law. Despite this, we persist in "getting tough on kids," in some collective hope our society will be safer as a result. Such a policy response to kids who break the law is misguided in several respects, mainly in that it assumes that punishment will correct behaviour. Most kids who are in constant trouble with the law have been punished and abused in various ways throughout their lives; further punishment is morally wrongly and correctively ineffective. It assumes that child and youth crime is the result of criminal kids. Most kids in the justice system, however, have substantial physical and psychological health issues that are related to their actions. Lastly, punitive policies make the vengeful assumption, through the rhetoric of responsibility, that kids who break the law deserve what they get.

The programs that are successful with kids in trouble do not involve incarceration or punishment; they involve kindness, mentorship and often one-to-one care. The problem is that most politicians and the general public perceive such programs to be inordinately expensive and to be indulgent of the already incorrigible. In reality, the money spent on mentoring programs for kids in trouble pays off considerably — just not in the short term. The benefits accrue over the lifetime of the individual — in increased productivity, better health and less contact with the criminal justice system. The human rights-based goal that children and youth should be free from legal abuse is actually quite attainable; it takes, however, a considerable shift in our thinking about crime and punishment and a larger investment in childhood.

Freedom from Labour Discrimination

Children and youth who work for wages should receive the same financial and personal protections accorded all people who work. If we deny young people fundamental labour rights, then we are simply engaged in labour exploitation. This is not histrionics — this is human rights. We know that many if not most children and youth work during their school years. We also know that young people typically work in establishments that offer them no labour rights protection,

The discussions I put forth in Chapter 4 show clearly that, as a society, we do not uphold labour rights for the young and do, indeed, exploit their labour. Fast food multinational corporations, for example, depend on the part-time, unprotected labour of the young for maximum profit and do not meet what we would consider acceptable labour practices. The argument in support of young people working in such industries for wages and conditions inferior to those of adults is that they are inexperienced, are receiving support from their parents and consequently do not need to make a lot of money. We make the assumptions that they need to gain employment experience to prepare them for later on in life and that they need the flexibility to work around school. These seem like logical arguments, but they do not hold up when we consider that many adult entry-level jobs do not require experience, that many jobs throughout the work world are unskilled and that many young people do indeed need the money. Most families in the modern world depend on multiple earners. There is no reason, in fact, for us to exploit the labour of the young simply because of their age.

It would be relatively simple to rectify this situation by upholding labour standards for the young. The standards would include all of those things that adults expect in any job: on-the-job training, safety training, accident benefits, employment insurance, adequate wages, safe working conditions and the right to organize. Companies faced with upholding acceptable labour standards for their young employees may threaten to leave or shut down, and this has happened. However, if labour standards were uniformly enforced across the country, the threat would diminish rapidly because companies will not leave the entire consumer market. Further, most sound economic theory suggests that, in the long term, the decent treatment of employees results in greater loyalty and greater productivity.

The Right to Learn

Our universal system of public education is based on ensuring that all children have equal and adequate access to education. One of the persistent realities of education in Canada, however, is that educational success depends largely on social class and geography among other things. I entitled Chapter

5 "The Right to Learn" because our schools should be much more than places that simply pass on formal knowledge. They are the places in which young people spend a good part of their lives and, as such, need to be places of engagement and passion. There is an argument to be made that schools have become more like factories that produce students with grades attached to their names, grades upon which society judges their success. The problem is that when we discuss educational achievement, we are not talking about how well students are engaged in their schools and how they become active citizens; we are talking about marks and the school's reputation.

The empirical evidence in Chapter 5 shows clearly how fundamentally important school engagement is to the well-being of young people. High levels of school engagement enhance self-worth, contribute to physical and mental health, decrease anxiety, prevent contact with the criminal justice system and reduce substance abuse of all kinds. The right to go to a school that engages its students should be a fundamental human right. And, the possibility of dramatically enhancing school engagement does exist. The alternative schools I have studied that are successful in turning around the lives of marginalized kids engage students in profound ways. They focus on mentoring, safety, health, student involvement in curricula, student athletics as a core activity, student-to-student learning across grades and justice in place of punishment. They create, in short, an environment in which even the most damaged of children care to attend. This should be the goal for all education institutions, and there is a good argument to be made than when schools are places of comfort and care, the educational successes follow naturally.

The problem for society is that the school engagement model is expensive. To make schools liveable places for all young people, governments need to increase substantially the resources available for buildings, staff, regularized student support and care, and community involvement. Unfortunately, we have adopted a model of education funding that is so tied to the public purse that we cannot escape the ideology that education is a public expense and not a long-term public investment.

Freedom from Corporate Aggression

This last right, to be free from corporate aggression, brings up particularly troubling issues for us as a society for several reasons. First, we fundamentally believe that if something is bad for us, we should simply not buy it. Second, corporations engage in campaigns to help kids. They promote reading in school, they provide educational materials for schools, they do research and provide medical solutions for kids who are psychologically impaired, and they provide employment for the young that fits with the school day. The problem I discussed in Chapter 6 is that all of this corporate benevolence comes with a price, a price that our children have to pay. The darkest side of the price is that corporations have direct access to children and youth, who are, in essence, a captive audience for what is really advertising under the guise of philanthropy.

The human rights issue is quite clear. Adults have input into public policy through many channels including the voting booth, the administration of public and private organizations, and community-based activist groups. Adults are consumers and workers, but they are also political managers. Children and youth are consumers and workers but not political managers. In a position of political disenfranchisement, should children and youth be exposed to corporate aggression? Adults can resist through political machinery. Young people cannot.

How Well Are We Doing?

I think the best way to end this book is to ask us all to reflect on how well we are doing as a nation as we keep in mind our personal and public declarations of the welfare of the young as our most important pursuit. Canada is a signatory to the *United Nations Convention on the Rights of the Child*, a binding document that demands that we uphold our declared position that no child should suffer. It stands as the benchmark for Canadian society. Given what we have encountered in this book, we must decide whether we are living up to our commitments. I end with the declaration Canada signed and to which we as individuals need constantly to renew our pledge to uphold.

Core Principles on the United Nations Convention on the Rights of the Child

The Convention on the Rights of the Child is the first legally binding international instrument to incorporate the full range of human rights — civil, cultural, economic, political and social rights. It spells out the basic human rights that children everywhere have: the right to survival; to develop to the fullest; to protection from harmful influences, abuse and exploitation; and to participate fully in family, cultural and social life. The four core principles of the Convention are non-discrimination; devotion to the best interests of the child; the right to life, survival and development; and respect for the views of the child. Every right spelled out in the Convention is inherent to the human dignity and harmonious development of every child. The Convention protects children's rights by setting standards in health care; education; and legal, civil and social services.

By agreeing to undertake the obligations of the Convention (by ratifying or acceding to it), national governments have committed themselves to protecting and ensuring children's rights and they have agreed to hold themselves accountable for this commitment before the international community. States parties to the Convention are obliged to develop and undertake all actions and policies in the light of the best interests of the child.

Source: Excerpted from the *UNICEF Convention on the Rights of the Child* (1990) <http://www.unicef.org/crc/>.

NOTES

Chapter 1

1. Statistics Canada, 2007, *Canada Survey of Giving, Volunteering and Participating* (Ottawa: Government of Canada).

2. The World Bank, 2001, *The World Development Report 2000/2001: Attacking Poverty* (New York: Oxford University Press).

3. UNICEF, 2010, *The Children Left Behind: A League Table of Inequality in Child Well-Being in the World's Richest Countries, Report Card 9* (Florence, Italy: The Innocenti Research Centre).

4. National Council of Welfare, 2007, *Poverty Profile 2007* (Ottawa: National Council of Welfare), Reports No. 4.

5. J. Gronick and M. Jantii, 2009, *Child Poverty in Upper Income Countries: Lessons from the Luxembourg Income Study* (Luxembourg: Luxembourg Income Study).

6. National Council of Welfare, 2007, *Poverty Profile 2007*.

7. Geoffrey York, 1992, *The Dispossessed: Life and Death in Native Canada* (Toronto: Little, Brown).

8. Helen Cote and Wendy Schissel, 2008, "Damaged Children and Broken Spirits: A Residential School Survivor's Story," in Carolyn Brooks and Bernard Schissel (eds.), *Marginality and Condemnation: An Introduction to Criminology*, second edition (Halifax, NS: Fernwood Publishing); Jim Miller, 1996, *Shingwauk's Vision: A History of Native Residential Schools* (Toronto: University of Toronto Press).

9. Aboriginal Healing Foundation, 1999, *Program Handbook* (Ottawa: Aboriginal Healing Foundation).

Chapter 2

1. G. Egaland, A. Pacey, Z. Cao, and I. Sobol, 2010, "Food Insecurity Amongst Inuit Preschoolers: Nunavut Inuit Child Health Survey, 2007–2008," *Canadian Medical Association Journal* 182 (3), pp. 243–48.
2. Darcy Frey, 2004, *The Last Shot: City Streets, Basketball Dreams* (New York: Mariner Books).
3. Eric Schlosser, 2002, *Fast Food Nation: The Dark Side of the All-American Meal* (New York: Perennial).
4. Tamar Lewin, 2010, "If Your Kids Are Awake, They're Probably Online," *New York Times Online*, January 20.
5. Victoria J. Rideout, G. Foehr, and D.F. Roberts, 2010, *Generation M2: Media in the Lives of 8 to 18 Year Olds* (Mungo Park, CA: Kaiser Family Foundation).
6. Richard Louv, 2006, *Last Child in the Woods: Saving Our Children from Nature Deficit Disorder* (Chapel Hill: Algonquin Books of Chapel Hill).
7. Health Canada, *Reaching for the Top: A Report by the Advisor on Healthy Children and Youth* (Ottawa: Health Canada, 2009).
8. K. Leitch, 2007, "Reach for the Top: A Report by the Advisor on Healthy Children and Youth," Ottawa: Health Canada.
9. Canadian Children's Rights Council, 2003, *Youth Suicide Report — Canadian Task Force on Preventive Health Care* (Ottawa: Canadian Children's Rights Council).
10. Canadian Population Health Initiative, 2005, *Improving the Health of Young Canadians* (Ottawa: Canadian Institute for Health Information).
11. K. Sternheimer, 2006, *Kids These Days: Facts and Fictions About Today's Youth* (Lanham, MD: Rowman & Littlefield).
12. Society of Obstetricians and Gynecologists of Canada, 2006, *Sex Facts in Canada, 2006* (Ottawa: Society of Obstetricians and Gynecologists of Canada).
13. Society of Obstetricians and Gynecologists of Canada, 2006. *Sex Facts*.
14. Craig Watkins, 2006, *Hip Hop Matters: Politics, Pop Culture, and the Struggle for the Soul of a Movement* (Boston, MA: Beacon Press) pp. 219.
15. Lisa Tremblay, 2010, "The New Sexual Exploitation," *Herizon*, Fall.

Chapter 3

1. For an extended discussion of the public demonization of young offenders, see Bernard Schissel, 2006, *Still Blaming Children: Youth Conduct and the Politics of Child Hating* (Halifax: Fernwood Publishing).
2. Janice Tibbetts, 2009, "Canada's Youth Crime Laws Hailed as Success," *National Post* <http://www.nationalpost.com/news/story.html?id=2207627>.

3. *Report of the Manitoba Aboriginal Justice Inquiry*, 1999 <http://www.ajic.mb.ca/volume.html>.
4. The Saskatchewan Commission on First Nations and Métis Peoples and Justice Reform, 2004.
5. The Saskatchewan Commission on First Nations and Métis Peoples and Justice Reform, 2004.

Chapter 4

1. Statistics Canada, 2009, *Canadian Youth in Transition Survey, 2006–2007* (Ottawa: Statistics Canada).
2. Eric Schlosser, 2002, *Fast Food Nation: The Dark Side of the All-American Meal* (New York: Perennial).
3. Michel Arsenault, 2008, "Child's Play: Why Hasn't Quebec Re-Established a Minimum Age for Employment?" *Walrus Magazine*, Oct/Nov, pp. 26–28.
4. Sandra Rollings-Magnuson, 2009, *Heavy Burdens on Small Shoulders: The Labour of Pioneer Children on the Canadian Prairies* (Edmonton, AB: University of Alberta Press).
5. B. Barnetson, 2009, "Regulation of Child and Adolescent Employment in Alberta," *Just Labour: A Canadian Journal of Work & Society*, 13, pp. 29–47.
6. Steven Greenhouse, 2010, "The Unpaid Intern, Legal or Not," *New York Times*, April 2, <http://www.nytimes.com/2010/04/03/business/03intern.html>.
7. And, most often, injuries like burns and scalds and typical agriculture-related injuries go unreported.
8. Statistics Canada, 2009, *Canadian Youth in Transition*.
9. For a comprehensive historical readings on residential schools, see Jim Miller, 1996, *Shingwauk's Vision: A History of Native Residential Schools* (Toronto: University of Toronto Press); and John S. Molloy, 1999, *A National Crime: The Canadian Government and the Residential School System — 1879 to 1986* (Winnipeg, MB: University of Manitoba Press).
10. A. Prentice, 1977, *The School Promoters* (Toronto: McClelland and Stewart).

Chapter 5

1. E.M. Thomas, 2009, *Canadian Nine-Year-Olds at School* (Ottawa: Statistics Canada).
2. A. Nikiforuk, 2008, *Tar Sands: Dirty Oil and the Future of a Continent* (Vancouver: Greystone Books); T. Clarke, 2008, *Tar Sands Showdown: Canada and the New Politics of Oil in an Age of Climate Change* (Toronto:

James Lorimer).

3. Michael Corbett, 2007, *Learning to Leave: The Irony of Schooling in a Coastal Community* (Halifax, NS: Fernwood Publishing).

4. Statistics Canada, 2009, *Canadian Youth in Transition Survey, 2006–2007* (Ottawa: Statistics Canada).

5. Canadian Labour Force Survey, 2007, *Provincial Drop-Out Rates: Trends and Consequences* (Ottawa: Statistics Canada).

6. B. Schissel and T. Wotherspoon, 2003, *The Legacy of School for Aboriginal People: Education, Emancipation and Oppression* (Don Mills, ON: Oxford).

Chapter 6

1. Carly Weeks, 2010, "Energy Drinks Post a Serious Health Threat to Kids: Canadian Medical Journal," *Globe and Mail*, Monday, July 26, <http://www.theglobeandmail.com/life/health/energy-drinks-pose-serious-health-risk-to-kids-canadian-medical-journal/article1652080/>.

2. D.A. Christakis, F.J. Zimmerman, D.L. DiGuiseppe and C.A. McCarty, 2004, "Early Television Exposure and Subsequent Attentional Problems in Children," *Pediatrics* 113 (4), pp. 708–13.

3. Eric Schlosser, 2005, *Fast Food Nation: The Dark Side of the All-American Meal* (New York: Harper Perennial).

4. Richard Louv, 2006, Last Child in the Woods: Saving Our Children from Nature Deficit Disorder (Chapel Hill: Alconquin Books).

5. S.R. Flora and D.B. Flora, 1999, "Effects of Extrinsic Reinforcement for Reading During Childhood on Reported Reading Habits of College Students," *Psychological Record* 49, pp. 3–14.

6. Cheng Ye Ji and Tsung O. Cheng, 2009, "Epidemic Increase in Overweight and Obesity in Chinese Children from 1985 to 2005," *International Journal of Cardiology*, 132, 1 (6), pp. 1–10.

7. A. Sutherland and B. Thompson, 2003, *Kidfluence: The Marketer's Guide to Understanding and Reaching Generation Y — Kids, Tweens, and Teens* (New York: McGraw-Hill).

8. Juliet Shor, 2004, *Born to Buy: The Commercialized Child and the New Consumer Culture*. New York: Scribner.

Chapter 7

1. Bernard Schissel, 2006, *Still Blaming Children: Youth Conduct and the Politics of Child Hating* (Halifax, NS: Fernwood Publishing).

ACKNOWLEDGEMENTS

I am indebted to many people for their support, encouragement and skills. First, I would like to express my gratitude to the Office of Research at Royal Roads University for their support and financial assistance and to my research assistant, Karen Charlebois.

To Errol Sharpe and the staff at Fernwood Publishing, my thanks for their support and continuing efforts to provide relevant, important, and accessible publications. Their ongoing commitment to social justice inspires exemplary writing and I congratulate them for their vision in creating this *About Canada* series. I would especially like to thank Wayne Antony for his sound guidance, his editorial expertise, and his ongoing commitment to thoughtful and reflective publishing. To Brenda Conroy for copy editing, Beverly Rach and Debbie Mathers for production and layout, and John van der Woude for designing the cover, my gratitude. Thanks also to the anonymous reviewers for comments on the draft.

Lastly, I would like to thank Wendy for her unwavering support, her intellectual guidance and her exceptional editorial skills.

ABOUT CANADA

From health care to agriculture, childcare, globalization, immigration, energy, water and more: the books in this series explore key issues for Canadians. About Canada books provide basic — but critical and passionate — coverage of central aspects of our society. Written in accessible language by experts in their fields, the books are presented in a popular format, at affordable prices.

Forthcoming — Fall 2011

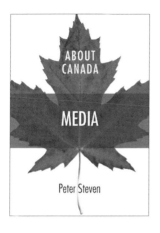

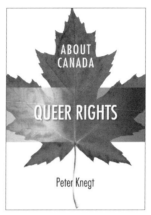

.

About Canada: Immigration

Nupur Gogia & Bonnie Slade

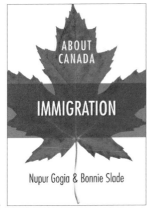

pb 9781552664070 pb $17.95
hb 9781552664315 hb $34.95
144pp Rights: World March 2011

Many Canadians believe that immigrants steal jobs away from qualified Canadians, abuse the healthcare system and refuse to participate in Canadian culture. In *About Canada: Immigration,* Gogia and Slade challenge these myths with a thorough investigation of the realities of immigrating to Canada. Examining historical immigration policies, the authors note that these policies were always fundamentally racist, favouring whites, unless hard labourers were needed. Although current policies are no longer explicitly racist, they do continue to favour certain kinds of applicants. Many recent immigrants to Canada are highly trained and educated professionals, and yet few of them, contrary to the myth, find work in their area of expertise. Despite the fact that these experts could contribute significantly to Canadian society, deeply ingrained racism, suspicion and fear keep immigrants out of these jobs. On the other hand, Canada also requires construction workers, nannies and agricultural workers — but few immigrants who do this work qualify for citizenship. *About Canada: Immigration* argues that we need to move beyond the myths and build an immigration policy that meets the needs of Canadian society.

NUPUR GOGIA received her PhD in sociology and equity studies in education at OISE, University of Toronto. BONNIE SLADE is a research fellow with the Institute of Education at the University of Stirling in Scotland.

www.fernwoodpublishing.ca

About Canada: Health and Illness

Dennis Raphael

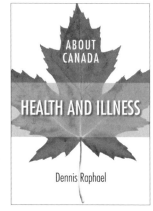

pb 9781552663752 pb $17.95 hb 9781552663882 hb $34.95 172pp 2010

This book argues that it is the social determinants of health, imposed on us by the "market," that dictate the health of Canadians. Social determinants include such things as income and wealth, employment, quality of education, access to health and social services and ability to obtain food and housing. Dennis Raphael compellingly demonstrates that the health and longevity of Canadians could be greatly improved not by changes to lifestyle, but through simple changes to social policy.

About Canada: Health Care

Pat Armstrong & Hugh Armstrong

pb 9781552662465 $17.95 160pp 2008

For more than 30 years, Canadians have enjoyed high quality health care based on need and not on ability to pay. This book explains how the Canadian system works and assesses reforms underway.

www.fernwoodpublishing.ca

About Canada:
Animal Rights
John Sorenson

pb 9781552663561 $17.95 192pp 2010

This book analyzes discourses used by animal-exploitation industries to defend their practices and suggests that a society that claims to protect animals while maintaining antiquated laws is suffering from "moral schizophrenia."

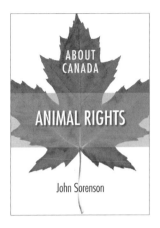

About Canada:
Childcare
Martha Friendly
& Susan Prentice

pb 9781552662915 $17.95 150pp 2009

"Students will get the 'big picture' of ECEC issues, politics and policy in Canada and learn what should be done to build a well-designed publicly funded universal system—there isn't another book that does this."
— *Rachel Langford, Ryerson University*

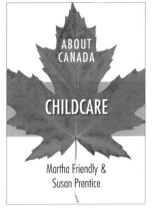

www.fernwoodpublishing.ca

0 1341 1378769 8